5/3/97

To Mim and Miles

With my best wishes,

Happiness always

Alice Kaufer

GOODBYE FOR ALWAYS

THE TRIUMPH OF THE INNOCENTS

GOODBYE FOR ALWAYS

THE TRIUMPH OF THE INNOCENTS

BY CECILE KAUFER AND JOE ALLEN

© 1997 by Cecile Kaufer and
Joseph Allen
All Rights Reserved

Produced by E.L. Smith, Inc.

Cover and book designed
by Ann Byne

About this cover: Remnants of
a family's history become
woven together in a collage,
with overlapping images of
Cecile's childhood.

Special thanks to Ann Byne of
Byne Graphics for her inspira-
tional design of the cover and
the body of this book.

Special thanks to Hilton I.
Kaufman for the printing of
"Good-Bye for Always, The
Triumph of the Innocents."

Special thanks to Arthur
Stanton, Jr. for his contribution
to the production process.

Special thanks to Robert
Socolof for his editing of
the manuscript.

Photos courtesy of The
Rockland Center for Holocaust
Studies and The Cecile
Widerman Kaufer Collection.

Published by Hudson Cove
Publishing, Tomkins Cove, NY

Printed in The United States of
America

Library of Congress Catalog
Card Number: 97-73795

ISBN 1-890975-18-4

For Herz, Laja and Marguerite Widerman,
for whom love shines ever brightly,
undiminished by the passage of time.

For Gene Allen, whose spirit and love of life continues to live on in those he touched.

For future generations of young people, who will become untouched by personal experiences of the Holocaust. May they never know the deep, searing pain of that time, but always remember those before them who did.

FOREWORD

In 1942, the City of Paris was actually two cities in one.

It was still as beautiful as ever. The cobblestone avenues were tree-lined and familiar. The apartments and office buildings still stood straight up, seemingly to the sky, proud in their look and feel. When you looked at them, they still said "home."

Paris was a special place. Millions of people called it home. It had a history that seemed to spill from each stone. The city possessed the magical combination of hustle and bustle along with a special warmth, wrapping its arms around each person in safety and security. It was a place that belonged to all who lived there.

But in 1942 Paris was a different city as well. Some two years before, the Nazis had forced their way into the lives of Parisians and the pain of their presence was everywhere. On every street, around every corner, virtually anywhere you looked, you could see them. Nazi soldiers in the street made the city frightening. Like a disease infecting the body, the soldiers were invading the very flesh of Paris, just as they had been invading cities throughout Europe.

They were terrifying. When they looked at you, they made you turn your head in fear. They seemed to actually enjoy instilling terror in everyone. No one who lived in Paris could be sure that when they left their homes, they would return.

Many of the offices and other buildings we knew so well had become the headquarters of a Nazi organization. It made you cry to see soldiers and Nazi officials standing in hallways or peering through windows of what once belonged to us.

Through it all, Paris still possessed its strong and beautiful body. However, the Nazis had clearly stolen its soul.

It was worse for Jews than it was for anyone else. The Nazis hated Jews, we knew that. That made Jews more frightened than anyone else. All Parisians had to put up with invaders in their midst, but we Jews had to put up with the fact that we were hated and easy targets. The Nazis were hard on Jews, you could see it every day. Almost daily, there were scenes of groups of soldiers beating a young man in an alley or courtyard. You could see people walking down the street suddenly being stopped and taken away. Later on, we would almost always find out the poor soul was Jewish and sometimes he would never be seen again.

Everyone, even an 11 year old child, could feel the danger in the air. People would speak in whispers when they talked about the Nazis and usually left those conversations to times when they were safely inside with people they knew. It was dangerous to speak openly of the Nazis. It could get you taken away. Anyone who spoke too loudly or discussed the occupation in public would soon be gone.

So the talk of the Nazis and their bitter occupation began to disappear beneath the surface. However, the feeling of fear and dread did not. The adults tried to make the children feel that everything was the same as it always was. The children were simply able to "feel" that life was different—and not for the better. A sadness came over people in every neighborhood and walking quickly with heads bowed became the order of the day.

Shortly after the Nazis arrived, they made all Jews come into their new offices and informed us we would have to wear yellow Stars of David to identify us as Jews. It made all of us different and we stood out like poor sore thumbs. This made life worse. So many Christians were getting caught up in the growing wave of anti-Semitism that they were happy to do the Nazis' bidding. They were encouraged to make the Jews outsiders. Protestants and Catholics we had known as friends were now willing to taunt and tease us in the street. It was no better when we went to school. The teachers took our books away and made us sit in the back of the room. We were always disciplined harshly for even the smallest things and our classmates who weren't Jewish seemed to enjoy the hard lot we had in school. Our friends stopped being our friends. Their parents were telling them that Jews were bad and needed to be yanked out of French culture. I didn't know if they were doing this because they truly hated us or because they thought the Nazis would be easier on them if they did it. Whatever the reason, school had become a chamber of horrors for Jewish children.

No matter how bad it was to live in Paris, it got much worse when they made my father leave the city and go to work far away cutting down trees. Many of the Jewish men in our neighborhood had to leave their jobs and their families and go away. We didn't know where they were going or when they would be back. Our mothers told us they would be home soon and all of us would be together again, but it was sometimes easy to see that our mothers weren't sure of what they were saying. The children prayed that their fathers would come back to them.

Without the men, our neighborhoods took on a new look. Our mothers or our grandparents had to do everything—take care of us, try to find some kind of work in order to afford food and tell us over and over that this was only temporary. Everyone wanted to believe them, some of us even did.

Three months after my father went away he wrote and told us he and the others were going to be allowed to come home. Their work cutting down trees in the woods so far away was soon ending and he would be returning. That uplifted our spirits and encouraged us to believe that everything would be all right once again. We didn't think that the Nazis would be leaving anytime soon, but with our families all together again we felt we would be able to somehow put up with them.

The men returned much different than when they left. They were all exhausted and the look in their eyes had changed. Each of the men had seen a little bit of the future. They knew some of what the Nazis were capable of and what they didn't or couldn't say was every bit as important as what they did say. Some of the children overheard the stories of the men being beaten by guards for not working hard enough, or fast enough or for no reason. Some of the men had even been shot by guards who said they were trying to escape.

Still, in many neighborhoods in the city, there was a feeling of joy. Yes, things had gotten worse, that much was true. In fact, many Jewish children now were not allowed or too afraid to even go to school. Many Jewish shops and businesses had been closed down or taken over by the Nazis. This put many people out of work and the struggle to feed families was worse than ever. What the men came home to was a community that was slowly being removed from the rest of the society. Seven months ago, the first Jews were taken away and brought to a prison. We didn't know much about it then. No one did.

But with fathers home and there for their children at night, the fear was lessened. Life went on—however narrow it was.

Yes, Paris was two cities in one that summer of 1942. It was a city with its heart removed. Much of it looked the same as it always did, but when you peered a little closer you would have seen it had changed. That change was evident in all aspects of life in the city. The country had been defeated. The conquerors were among us, taking whatever they wanted. For the Jews, that would mean giving up everything—each and every part of their lives now belonged to the Nazis and even that wasn't enough for them. Simply owning the lives of the Jews did not satisfy them. There would be a next step. No one living in the City of Lights could know what that next step would be. But it was coming.

Chapter One

"Cecile, Betty, come on children. Time for bed," Laja called to the back room where the girls were playing.

"In a minute, Mama," Cecile called back.

Laja could hear the sound of laughter coming from the back room of the tiny, three room apartment. It was the most beautiful sound she could hear and she didn't push them to stop. She stopped folding the wash so that she could just listen to it. It wasn't that she hadn't heard it before, it was just that she hadn't heard it much lately.

"Herz, listen to the girls," she said, turning to her husband who was busily writing a letter on the table. Betty's giggling was almost like music to her ears.

Herz looked in the direction of the room. "I hate to have them go to sleep. It's so nice to hear their voices."

"I know, but it's late and they ought to be in bed. Come on, my darlings, bedtime."

Both Cecile and Betty burst into the front room Cecile was 11 years old and was clearly in charge of the game. She was small for her age, but always filled with energy. From the time Herz and Laja could remember, Cecile wanted to play, or sing or simply run around. Her brown hair was cut short and bangs fell across her forehead. It seemed every time Cecile wasn't running around, she was standing with her hands on her hips, waiting to bark out the next set of orders.

She was chasing six year old Betty, who was laughing robustly as she ran trying to avoid Cecile. Betty jumped right on top of Herz' lap in her effort to get away. Betty was shy and seemed willing to watch Cecile set the pace. However, when Betty smiled, her eyes lit up the room like a spotlight.

"Papa, Cecile is trying to catch me. Papa."

Cecile crossed Herz' lap from the opposite side. "Now I have you." She began to tickle the younger girl until high pitch squeals filled the tiny apartment.

"All right, all right. Calm down. Shh, shh, quiet down." He said as he held each girl in one arm. "Marguerite will be home any minute and we don't want you to be up when she comes home."

"Papa, will Henri be coming home with her?" Cecile asked.

"Oh yes, he'll be bringing her home but he will have to leave to go to his home too."

Marguerite was almost a goddess to Cecile. She was 18 and exquisitely beautiful. She was engaged to be married to a wonderful young man named Henri and all the talk of marriage and weddings was a fantasy to a child with precious few fantasies left.

"I want to stay up until Marguerite and Henri come home," Cecile pleaded.

"I want to stay up too," Betty said with equal passion.

"I'm sorry girls, it is bedtime now. It is getting very late and I want you to get your sleep. Herz, tell them it is bedtime."

"Mama is right, my darlings. It is time for bed. Come, I'll bring you." He lifted both girls up and brought them over to where Laja was sitting. "Give Mama a wonderful kiss and say I love you."

"I love you Mama," Cecile said as she reached from her father's grasp to wrap her arms around her mother's neck."

"Good night Cecile," Laja said, giving her middle daughter a kiss on the lips. "Good night Betty," she smiled into her youngest daughter's eyes, almost drinking in her reflection. "Sleep sweetly." Betty returned her kiss and didn't want to let go.

Herz brought the girls to their bed and gently laid them in it. The fidgeting continued as they tried to find the right spots for sleep. Cecile tried to take the bulk of the blanket while Betty fought to keep some for herself.

"Good night Papa," Cecile said.

"Good night Papa," Betty echoed. Betty almost always echoed Cecile.

"Sleep well, girls. I will see you in the morning. You can tell me about your dreams." He always wanted to hear about their dreams, whether they actually had them or not.

He turned from their bed and came out to Laja. "It's not getting too late for Marguerite, is it?"

"She'll be back soon, Herz" Laja said barely looking up. "I think I'm going to get ready for bed, too."

"All the same, I'll wait for her. I don't like her to be out anyway."

Laja placed the clothes into the drawers, stretched and walked into the hall to the bathroom. Even with the bathroom outside the apartment and down the hall, she could still hear the girls whispering from their bed.

It didn't take Marguerite long to arrive home. She and Henri walked in moments after Laja walked out. Herz put his finger to his lips as they walked to the door and pointed to where the girls were trying to fall asleep.

"The girls are sleeping," he whispered.

Both Henri and Marguerite responded, each putting their fingers to their lips.

"How are you, Papa?" Marguerite asked, as if she hadn't seen him in days rather than the three hours since she and Henri went out. They had spent the evening at his house, just a short distance away. It was a time for celebration for the young couple, despite what was going on in the city. They were hoping the Nazi occupation would be over before their marriage but they were willing to go ahead with it, occupation or not. Henri's parents had even thrown them a small engagement party not long ago.

"Did you have any trouble coming home?" Herz asked.

"No Papa, we barely saw any soldiers out tonight."

"How are your parents, Henri?"

"They're fine, Mr. Widerman. They asked to send their regards to you."

Laja returned from the bathroom in her robe. She looked very ready to go to sleep. "How nice to see you Henri." She turned to Marguerite. "Hello my darling. I'm glad you're home."

Henri said he ought to be going back home. Marguerite walked to the door arm in arm with him.

"Be careful going home, Henri. Remember that group of men we saw on the avenue.

"Don't worry, Marguerite. I will be fine. I'll come by tomorrow night for you.

"I love you Henri," Marguerite said as he opened the door. Herz in the corner rolled his eyes in the direction of his wife.

"I, uh, love you too, Marguerite. Good night Mr. Widerman. Good night Mrs. Widerman. I'll see you tomorrow."

Laja and Herz both waved to the young man as he closed the door behind him.

Marguerite seemed to light up the room as she buzzed by. At 18, she was nearly an adult and an absolute joy to Herz and Laja. Since they arrived from Poland 16 years earlier, Marguerite was at the center of their lives. She did very well in school. She was popular in the neighborhood and as she got into her teens, was a magnet for young men.

Laja and Herz were both quite strict with their older daughter and that strictness paid off as she closed in on adulthood. A beautiful, mature, happy young woman, she was all her parents could ask for. They only hoped the occupation would somehow end before they were all swallowed up in the madness around them.

Marguerite walked out the door and went down the hall to the bathroom.

"Well, another day finished, Herz," Laja said letting a long breath out. "Let's hope tomorrow is another one."

"It will be, Laja. I think I will go and see Mr. Beauchamp about that suit he wanted." Before he was taken away to the woods, Herz was a tailor. He was now trying to go back to his trade, even though fewer and fewer people had money for clothes. At best, people were seeking him out for repairs. It made him far less money than new clothes would bring but every little bit would help. Mr. Beauchamp had asked him to drop by for a new suit just after he returned from the woods and he was anxious not to let the opportunity go by.

"Good, Herz. If he wants a new suit, perhaps we can take some of the money and buy the engagement present for Marguerite."

"I don't know if we can, Laja. We need so much and it's harder and harder to get by. We may have to wait for that. I'm sure they will understand. Henri's parents are in the same position, especially since the party."

"I know, but I think that children planning a wedding should be able to get some gifts. They'll have so many things to pay for. Think about it, darling. Let's see what we can do."

Laja turned back the blankets and crawled into bed. Herz waited for Marguerite to come back from the bathroom and then walked down the hall.

"How do you feel today, Mama?" Marguerite asked.

"I feel fine today. I'm coughing a little bit, but I'm feeling better."

Marguerite didn't really believe Laja. She had been battling tuberculosis and the coughing and wheezing that came along with it had become part of the household symphony.

"Just please take it easier, Mama. I worry about you."

"Thank you darling. I'll be fine."

"Papa seems happy tonight. Is he?"

"Oh yes. The little ones lift his spirit so much. If they don't make him go back to the woods he will be fine."

Marguerite took the little yellow Star of David off her dress as she hung it up and put it on her other dress. She had gotten used to changing it every evening before she went to bed so she wouldn't forget to do it in the morning when she went out.

Herz came back into the room and crawled into the bed.

"I am tired tonight. I think I'll sleep well. I hope you have a good night, Laja. Is your medicine on the table?"

"Oh yes. But I don't think I'll really need it. I've felt pretty well all day."

"Good night Marguerite," he said to his eldest daughter, the apple of his eye. "Sleep well, my darling."

"Thank you Papa. You sleep well too. I love you."

Herz thought it was wonderful that the last words spoken in the room were "I love you." Yes, he told himself, it was a nice way to end the day.

The room grew dark in the Widerman house. The sounds of night remained outside. Herz and Laja tried very hard to keep the insanity of the city out of their home so that the girls would always feel safe. No matter what happened in the streets, at home they were still the same close family, sharing the same love and appreciation for each other they always had. Laja and Herz were raising three wonderful children and whatever the Nazis would do, their caring for each other would remain untouched. Someday, this would be over and the couple hoped that it would not steal Marguerite's young adulthood or Cecile and Betty's childhood. They would do what they could to prevent that.

As midnight approached and July 11 turned into July 12, a peacefulness prevailed in the three tiny rooms and a quiet drifting off to sleep could be felt in each of them. The morning, as it always did, would be arriving soon.

Chapter Two

I t was 3:00 am in the morning of July 12, when a violent pounding on the front door woke the entire family.

"Open this door in the name of the law or we'll break it down!" a man's voice shouted at them. The pounding on the door continued.

"I said 'open it up or we'll break it down'."

Herz and Laja jumped out of sleep and immediately knew what was happening. Especially since they could also hear pounding on other doors in the building.

"It's them," Herz said.

"Oh my God," was all that Laja was able to say before she began to panic. "The girls."

"This is your last chance. Open the door." The voice outside the door was convincing.

"Laja, you open the door, I'll get the girls." He jumped out of bed, quickly threw on some clothes and ran into where the girls were sleeping. They were already up and very frightened.

Laja went to open the door. There were three soldiers standing outside and as soon as the door opened they forced their way in. Laja could see that this same scene was taking place at apartments throughout the floor.

The soldiers burst past Laja and once in the apartment screamed at her.

"Get your bags, you filthy Jews and hurry yourselves. We are taking you away and if you don't make it fast it will be the end of you."

Herz brought the girls into the sitting room and saw that the soldiers were pointing their guns at them. They continued to scream at the family to get moving.

"What have we done?" Herz pleaded. "What have we done?"

"Just shut up and get moving. You have three minutes to get out or we'll shoot you."

Cecile grabbed onto her father's leg. "Papa, what is happening? Papa, what do they want?"

"Shh, just do as they say." His face showed the fear and his words did nothing to console his middle daughter.

Laja rushed for a valise and began jamming things into it. There was little sense to what she was putting into it, she was just packing the first things she could get her hands on.

"Laja, put some clothes into the valise," Herz said. Laja had to take some of the things out of the valise in order to fit clothing in.

"What do they want, Herz?" Laja cried in Yiddish. "Where are they taking us?"

"Don't ask any questions. Just do as they say. They'll shoot us right here in front of the girls."

Marguerite was trying to help Laja place clothing into the shabby suitcase. One of the soldiers was leering at Marguerite. "Move faster, Jew," he said right into her eyes.

Marguerite wouldn't back down. "Where are you taking us?"

"None of your business. I am going to hurt you very badly if you don't hurry up."

Marguerite stepped back in fear and began to cry, she knew he meant what he said.

Herz picked up Cecile while Laja took a crying Betty in her

arms. Marguerite took the suitcase. As Herz passed the first German soldier, Cecile yelled at him.

"Why are you doing this to us? Go away and go back to your own country and leave us alone." The soldier spit at Cecile and slapped her hard across the cheek and was about to do so again when Herz pushed himself and Cecile into the hallway. Cecile was screaming in pain and fear.

Most of the people from the building were running down the stairs with soldiers right behind them, guns at their backs. Some of the light bulbs in the hallway had been smashed and parts of it were totally black with darkness. The soldiers were screaming as the panicked families pushed out into the street. Parents tried to make sure their families were together as they feared they would be trampled if any one of them failed to keep up.

Laja and Herz ran hurriedly down the steps with their youngest children in their arms. Marguerite could barely get down with the valise that contained all that they now owned.

Before she left, Cecile put her little bag of pictures of her family in her pocketbook, a small one her parents gave to her at her last birthday, along with a little doll Mama had made by hand. She held onto it tightly as her father rushed down the stairs.

Once out in the street they saw hundreds of people streaming out of every building on the avenue. All were being followed by guards with rifles screaming at them as they moved. The guards jammed their rifles hard into the back of those who didn't move quickly enough.

Someone in front of Herz and Cecile had dropped a package and went to pick it up. One German guard and then another set upon him and repeatedly beat him with their rifle butts.

"Move Jew. Move Jew. If you don't move you will die," they yelled as they hit him.

Many people in the crowd were crying as they tried to keep up the pace the Germans had established. Every time the line slowed a little, the guards would kick whomever was in front of them. They kicked Herz many times as he struggled to keep Cecile in his arms. They kicked Laja and Marguerite as well. Some in the crowds couldn't help but look back at the apartment building they had just left. It would be the last time they would ever see their neighborhood.

Although it was nighttime, there were people lining the streets watching this parade of horror. They yelled at the people participating in this forced march.

"You dirty Jews. You are being taken away. Good for you," they yelled.

"You'll never come back, Jews."

Those that didn't yell at the marchers just stared at the scene. It may have occurred to them that the people who were being taken away were not just Jews, they were Frenchmen—countrymen, who were being rounded up and removed. But if it did occur to them, they didn't show it. They looked at the poor souls in the street as scapegoats. If the Nazis didn't take the Jews, perhaps they would start on the bulk of French citizens. Some must have thought how lucky they were not to be Jewish.

Many people in the line who had brought more than just the smallest suitcases were forced to abandon them in streets. The guards kicked their valises out of the way and as the line moved on, other guards would rummage through them and throw them onto the side of the road. For Marguerite, the family's valise was getting too heavy to carry and to run with.

"Papa, I can't carry this any longer."

Herz turned to Marguerite as he held Cecile.

"Marguerite, throw it down. Let it go."

"No Papa, I won't"

"Marguerite, throw it down. You can't carry it and run."

She tried to carry it for another block, but after 50 yards or so she realized that she would fall with exhaustion if she didn't abandon it. She began to cry and threw the valise onto the sidewalk. When Cecile could no longer walk, Herz picked her up and carried her for the rest of the way.

The Germans forced them to walk for more than an hour until they arrived at a truck depot. By the time they got there, there were already hundreds, maybe thousands jammed into the loading yard.

Once they were able to stop, Laja began to cough. She looked like she could barely breathe and her wheezing and coughing was making her barely able to stand up.

"Laja, put Betty down for a minute so you can rest your arms," Herz said to his wife.

"No. I can't let her down, they'll take her." Betty was sleeping in her mother's arms and seeing her with her eyes comfortably shut made Laja want to hold her ever more tightly.

"No they won't. You have to rest," but Laja would not wake the little girl in order to put her down.

It wasn't much easier for Herz. Carrying the larger and heavier Cecile for miles had pushed him to near exhaustion. He put his daughter down and sloped his shoulders as he stood.

"Are you all right, Papa?" Marguerite asked.

"Yes, yes, I'm fine. Are you alright."

"Yes, I'm good. We'll be able to rest here for awhile."

Marguerite looked around to see if there were people she knew, especially Henri. She wanted to walk around to try and find him, but she knew if she did, she would run the risk of being separated from the family. They needed her help with the two little ones. It was a terrible time for Marguerite, who wanted so badly to find her fiance.

Suddenly, Marguerite found a familiar face in the crowd.

"Robert!" she cried out. "Robert, we are here." She saw her father's brother Robert in the crowd. "Papa, Mama, it's Robert."

Herz' brother Robert was 18 years old, the same age as Marguerite. He made his way to Marguerite and they embraced each other and cried their eyes out. They fell to the ground, still hugging tightly and still in tears, each trying to console the other.

Soon Herz dropped to the floor as well, then Laja dropped to her knees, too. They huddled together and held onto each other like they'd never let go. Fear and exhaustion had gripped each of them tightly.

Herz asked Robert about their parents. He told him that they were not at home when the Germans came so they weren't rounded up. Marguerite and Laja were so sad that Robert was taken when he was alone.

"I'm happy to see all of you safe," Robert said.

"Were so happy to see you, too darling," Laja said, trying to fit words around her bitter cough.

More and more people were coming into the truck depot and it was getting horribly crowded. The sun came up, which helped to dim the effect of the huge searchlights on the crowd. Some of the people, especially the children, slept in their parents arms. Some of the adults tried to sleep as well.

It was about three hours later when dozens of trucks in a long gray line rolled down the street and into the depot. Everyone in the yard quickly got up and the panic that had characterized the early part of the morning came upon them again. As frightening as the wait in the depot was, seeing the trucks made them realize they were going to be taken somewhere much further away.

People were being herded onto the trucks until they were filled. There was no consideration of keeping families together. They were just jammed into the vehicles, which immediately sped away. Anyone who still had their suitcases were force to leave the bags in the yard. A huge pile of suitcases was forming in the center of the depot.

Laja was still carrying Betty as they approached the front of line to board the truck. Marguerite followed and Cecile stood in front of Herz, who walked directly in front of Robert.

Laja climbed the stairs of the truck, which was almost filled. Marguerite followed with Cecile. Just as Herz was about to board a guard came over and stopped the boarding.

"It's filled," he said to Herz. "You will wait for the next one."

"No, Papa, please. That's my Papa. Please let him come on," Cecile turned and yelled. Marguerite and Laja, already well into the truck started screaming too. A policeman who spoke French ordered Cecile to be quiet.

"Please, Mr., let my Papa come on," Cecile said back in French. "We can't go away from here without Papa."

The policeman took pity on the little girl. He quickly jumped onto the truck and took Cecile and placed her on the lap of a woman in the front row. He turned around and walked back down the stairs.

"One more," he yelled and grabbed Herz by the arm and put him on the truck. Herz jumped up onto the truck and the guards immediately closed the back. Cecile began calling for her father who scooped her up in his arms and brought her back to where Marguerite and Laja were sitting. He looked like he was about to have a heart attack, but at least he was with his family.

In the resolution of that crisis, lost for a moment was the fact that Robert had not made it onto the truck. Marguerite soon realized it and climbed over an old woman to the side of the truck, which had been closed up with wire. She saw him and burst into tears.

"Robert, Robert, come to us," she cried. He couldn't hear her. In fact he couldn't even see that she was calling out to him. As the truck pulled further down the road, they saw the young man standing at the front of the line as the next truck rolled into place. All alone, Robert was the first one on the next truck, but he was gone forever. No one would ever see him again, nor learn what happened to him.

As the truck carrying the Widermans drove off, they could hear the taunts of people yelling at them.

"Put the dirty Jews to the stake," some cried.

"Kill them. Kill the Jews."

"Leave them to us."

The truck was very noisy but the sounds of coming tragedy were as clear as a bell. Many of the women in the truck were crying, some wailing. Many of the men were praying, some of them bursting into tears as they prayed. Those who weren't praying stared ahead, their faces pale in their fear.

Some of the people took out bits of paper and wrote notes to those they left behind. They threw the papers out of the truck, hoping some kindly soul would pick up the papers and mail them to the addresses scrawled on them. Those efforts of desperation were signs that the people on the trucks had a pretty good idea they would not be returning.

After hours of driving, the trucks pulled up to a large sports stadium, the Velodome D'hiver (Winter Garden). Once each truck pulled up, guards would drag people off and set about separating families into groups. People were screaming out loud as they were separated, older men in one place, younger men and boys in another, old women over there and so on. When their truck came to the place reserved for unloading, Herz told his children to stay very close to each other.

"Listen to me, I am going to tell them that Mama is very sick. There is no one to care for her but us and she needs medication very badly. Maybe they will let us stay together or at least let some of us be together."

As Herz stepped down, the guard told him to go in one direction, and was preparing to have Laja go in another.

"We can't be separated. My wife is gravely ill. If we are separated she might die."

One look at Laja was enough to make him agree with Herz. The strain of the day on top of the tuberculosis had taken its toll on Laja and she looked terribly sick. The guard didn't seem to know what to do. He didn't want to be responsible for anyone dying just yet. But he knew what he was instructed to do.

"As long as we are here, won't you please let me tend to her?"

Herz pleaded.

The guard thought again as he looked at the others waiting to come off the truck. Another vehicle was pulling in and a decision needed to be made.

"Alright, you go over there, all of you," the guard said, pointing to the inside of the stadium. Herz tried to say something to him to thank him for his kindness, but the guard just shoved him aside.

Herz took a look at the stadium and thought that the higher they would be in the building, the less likely they were to draw the attention of guards.

"Come on, we're going upstairs."

There were no escalators so the five of them had to walk up the stairs to the top floor. Laja was growing weaker by the hour and was having a difficult time even walking on flat ground, let alone walking up deep stairs. But she did, with a great deal of help from Marguerite. Herz took charge of the two little girls.

They got to the top floor, found a section of vacant floor and laid down, exhausted, frightened and very hungry.

"Mama, can I have dinner," Betty said to Laja.

"Shh, Betty, Mama is resting. We'll have dinner a little later. We must try to take a nap now," Herz said. Marguerite was already starting to doze off. Laja was having a great deal of trouble breathing and each breath seemed to take everything out of her. Cecile fell asleep on one side of her father's lap. Betty did the same on the other. Herz leaned back against the wall to try and stay awake. He didn't know what would happen at the stadium and he felt it was important for one of them to be awake. But soon, he too, was out.

No one knew how long they slept. It could have been days for all they knew. As each one awoke, the pangs of hunger overwhelmed them. Herz kept telling his children that food was on the way, but he wondered how long he would be successful with that story.

In fact, two days passed before there was any sign of food. By the time there was any sign of food, they were nearly delirious in their hunger.

"Look, Papa, they are giving something away," Cecile yelled to her father. She was right, guards were coming by and giving old bread to the children. They wouldn't give anything to the adults, but their children were given some sustenance.

The guard gave Betty a piece of bread and she ate it greedily. He gave a piece to Cecile as well and she took a bite and let it sit in her mouth. She turned around to see who else was given a piece and she saw her parents just looking at her. They were hungry too, Cecile thought. She was determined to find them some bread as well.

Cecile jumped up and ran over to where the guard was giving out the bread.

"Please mister, I'm so hungry. May I have a piece of bread?" She opened her eyes as wide as she could.

But the guard must have recognized her.

"Hey, you already had some bread. What are you trying to do?" He pushed Cecile away and she fell backwards onto the concrete. She became furious at the guard and when she got back up she stared at him and then stuck her tongue out at him.

"How do you like that?" she said.

As soon as she stuck her tongue out, the guard was on her in an instant.

"I ought to kill you, you dirty little Jew," he said. He lined her up and kicked her in the stomach with his boot. She fell to the ground and opened a cut on her head. She began to bleed.

Herz ran to the scene. The guard was going to kick her again.

"Please, she's a little girl and she was hungry. I'll assure that she'll not do that again." He picked up his daughter and carried her to where the rest of the family was sitting. Cecile looked up at her father and started to cry. Herz bent his head down and kissed Cecile on both cheeks and her forehead.

Everyone in the stadium was resigned to sit and wait for something to happen. More and more people were arriving every few minutes and the stadium was getting packed far beyond capacity. Horrifying things began to happen with so many desperate people in one place. Everyone was starving and all assembled had the feeling they were being buried alive in a concrete tomb.

An infant had fallen or was thrown from the top level of the stadium. Its mother was trying to jump after the crushed infant but was being held back by others who had witnessed the horrible event. Two guards soon appeared and dragged off the wailing woman. No one ever saw her again.

Rumors had spread that German guards were dragging women off and doing horrible things to them. There were stories of guards beating some men to death who were begging for food. Many people started praying the prayer for the dead, all thinking the end was about to come.

After several days the guards began to pass out food and water to the people in the stadium. It was stale but nourishing and it kept people alive.

In the midst of the horror a miracle occurred. Herz and his family were huddled in the corner, trying to sleep when Marguerite jumped up.

"Henri!" she screamed. "Henri, Oh my God, it's you." She got up almost as if in disbelief.

The family was able to see Marguerite's young man rushing toward them and watched as he swooped Marguerite up in a desperate embrace.

"Henri where have you been? I was so worried sick about you. I thought I would never see you again."

"Marguerite, I love you. I have been looking all over this stadium for you."

"Where are your parents, Henri?"

"I don't know. They took them away when we got off the

truck. I haven't been able to find them yet."

"Oh Henri, I'm so glad to see you." They held each other so tightly, there was no room for anything, including the tragedy of the moment, between them.

"Nothing could keep me away from you. I'd find you wherever you'd go, my beautiful Marguerite."

Herz came over and gave Marguerite and her fiance a hug.

"Henri," Marguerite's father said tenderly. "We are so happy you are here."

Time in the stadium continued to pass and the adults began to try and find ways to amuse the children. Laja was falling in and out of consciousness so the effort fell to Herz.

He called Cecile over to him.

"Shepali, my darling," he said using her Yiddish name. "Let's sing our little song together." It was a beautiful little song called "Jattendrais," which was translated as "I Will Wait for You." Herz and Cecile would sing the song together on Sunday mornings, when there was no work to be done and the little girls would crawl into bed with their parents. It was a special song for both of them and Herz wanted Cecile to sing it now.

She sang it to him with tears in her eyes. It was such a wonderful and important song because it belonged to her and her father. But as she sang, her tears flowed and she was barely able to finish. But she tried hard and was able to finish every last word. When it was done Herz took her in his arms and gave her a long hug and a sweet, loving kiss.

"I love you, my Shepali. I will wait for you," Herz said through a teary smile.

Laja took a deep turn for the worse. She began to cough up blood and it appeared that she might die right in the stadium. Herz and Marguerite were not with Betty, Cecile and Laja at the time. Herz was trying to find some water for his wife and Marguerite had gone to look for food with Henri.

"What's wrong with her," a guard asked. Someone near them

said she had tuberculosis. He called for a doctor to come up. When he arrived Laja was bleeding quite heavily.

"This woman must be taken away. She's very sick. Take her downstairs."

"No," Laja said. "I'm fine right here."

"We are taking you downstairs for your own good," the doctor said.

Two guards took Laja downstairs while others took Cecile and Betty to the same place. Down in the infirmary, the two girls waited by their mother's side as the doctor examined her.

"This woman needs a hospital. If she doesn't go to a hospital she will not live long." He spoke to the guards at length and then he came back to Laja's bed with another guard.

"We are taking you to a hospital now. You need care and we cannot let you stay here with the others."

"I can't go," Laja pleaded. "My family. Please don't take my family away."

The guard told her that the little girls would be led away and cared for.

"Please, my girls were born in France. They are not immigrants. They have rights as French citizens. Please let them come with me. I won't go without them. I'd rather die here."

The guard and the doctor spoke again and then came back to her.

"Your children can go with you. You will be taken to the hospital and they will stay at the hospital with you until you are better." He turned to other guards and told them to put Laja and her daughters in the ambulance and locked the doors.

"What about Papa?" Cecile said. "What about my Papa?" The guards wouldn't answer her. They just shoved her and Betty in the back of the ambulance with Laja.

"Let's get these Jew bastards to the hospital so they can die there," the ambulance driver said to his assistant. The ambulance moved out through the basement of the stadium.

Cecile panicked when she thought of how frightened her father would be when he learned they were taken. How she wished she could put her arms around her father another time. She wished she could hug Marguerite and go to her wedding. She cried and cried as the ambulance drove through the gates. Betty was crying too, looking at Cecile for some answers. But what could Cecile tell her? After all she was just 11 years old.

Marguerite and Herz remained behind at the stadium. As the stadium grew smaller in the distance, Cecile looked and knew that her Papa and her sister were somewhere inside.

"Good-bye Papa, good-bye Marguerite," Cecile said, half to herself and half out loud. It would be years before Cecile and Betty would find out what happened to them.

Chapter Three

T he ride to the hospital was frightening for Laja, Cecile and Betty. The men in the front of the ambulance continued to say horrible things loud enough for them to hear.

"Why don't we just stop and kill them now?"

"I hope they operate on her without anesthesia."

"We'll soon be rid of these Jews. Then we'll go back and get some more."

It was very hard for Cecile to hear these things. She was afraid they would be killed before they got to the hospital. She was also afraid that her Mama would die before they got there. Then what would happen to her and Betty?

But more than anything else, she worried about her Papa and Marguerite. Laja must have worried, too, although she slipped in and out of consciousness. When she was awake she would moan and cry and call out to him. Then she would slip back into her sleep and leave Cecile and Betty alone.

The road from the stadium was filled with people. Many had signs telling the soldiers to round up more people. It was almost kind of a carnival out there. The people seemed happy that Jews were being rounded up and taken away.

Betty started to ask when Papa and Marguerite were going to come.

"Don't worry Betty," Cecile said. "They'll be here soon. They'll come to get us at the hospital. We just have to wait for them and take care of Mama."

"I'm scared, Cecile."

"I'm scared too, Betty."

They pulled into the gates of the hospital and drove to the back. As soon as they got to the rear entrance, two guards along with a doctor and a nurse opened the back door. They took the girls out of the ambulance and made them wait on the side. They pulled the stretcher that held Laja out of the back and put it on the ground.

"She is suffering from advanced tuberculosis and needs to be isolated," the one who appeared to be a doctor said.

"Put her in a locked room and no one sees her except the doctors and nurses," the guard said, holding his rifle on the group.

"What about the girls?" the nurse said.

"I don't care what you do with them. However, they are not to come near the woman and wherever you put them, make sure it is locked—tight."

The guards took Laja's stretcher and walked inside. Another guard stopped the girls from following it in.

"You stay here."

"I want my Mama," Betty cried out.

"Where are you taking my Mama? We want to come, too," Cecile cried out.

Just then, a nurse came over to Cecile and Betty and bent down so she was more their size.

"Don't worry children, Mama is being taken care of. You come with me and we'll find a place for you."

She was the first adult besides her parents who had spoken kindly to them since this whole horrible episode began. She took the girls inside the same door, but turned away from the corridor where Laja had been taken and walked upstairs.

They got to a hallway with a lot of individual rooms. A guard met them at one of the rooms and used his keys to open the door. The woman led Betty and Cecile into the room and was about to turn around to leave.

"Don't worry girls. Mama will be all right."

The nurse left and when she closed the door, the guard quickly locked the door behind them. Cecile and Betty could hear muffled voices on the other side warning everyone not to go inside without permission.

Cecile looked around the room. There was one bed and very little else. She ran to the window and looked out. There were bars on the window and she had to lift her head up so she could see around the iron. The paint had chipped off the walls in a number of spots and the cold gray paint had long since started to fade.

The girls were quiet for a long time.

"Where is Mama?" Betty finally asked Cecile.

"I don't know, maybe in a room downstairs."

"Why can't we be with Mama?"

"The doctors are making her better. We have to stay here while they do."

Cecile continued to look out the window. As she did she reached into the pocket of her dress. She took out her little pocket book, which held a few pictures and looked at them, but quickly put them back. It hurt too much to see them. She held her doll, the one she took from the apartment, which was still there. She remembered how Mama and Papa gave it to her on her birthday. For a moment, she remembered the games she played with the doll, making it speak in different voices in order to be a different person all the time. Sometimes the doll was a princess or an actress, or a singer. Sometimes it was even Mama talking to Cecile or Cecile talking to Mama.

As the little girl held the doll and looked out the window, she wished she could be any of those people she could make her doll be. Where was her Papa? Where was her older sister? Where was her Mama, or cousin Robert or Marguerite's Henri? She didn't know where they were or what would happen to them. Instead there were men with guns and people who yelled at them. Cecile wasn't used to being alone without any adults and she was quite scared as she watched the people move freely and quickly through the courtyard.

No one came into their room for a whole day. Cecile gave Betty the doll to play with and she just stared outside. Both girls were hungry and tired as night began to fall.

"When is our bedtime, Cecile?"

"I don't know Betty, but I think we should go to sleep soon. Maybe they will let us see Mama tomorrow and we wouldn't want to be tired, would we."

"I hope we see Mama tomorrow. I hope we see Papa and Marguerite, too."

"Maybe if we try to fall asleep and pray, we will."

"I'm hungry," Betty said.

"Me, too." They are probably giving all the food tonight to the very sick people. I'm sure they will give us breakfast in the morning." Cecile pulled the blanket down on the bed. The sheets were clean and the blanket wasn't too heavy.

"Betty, it's just like our bed at home. Let's try to go to sleep."

"I'm frightened," Betty said softly. "I don't want to go to sleep without Mama or Papa."

"I'm sure they are going to sleep, too. They are probably thinking about us right at this very moment. So come on, let's go to bed."

Both girls crawled into the bed and held onto each other very tightly. They could not turn the light off so the room had a yellow and orange glow against the night. As they quieted down, Betty began to cry. The past several days had been so hard for her and she was forced on so many occasions to act well beyond her years. Cecile tried to comfort her by holding her even tighter. While somewhat comforting for Betty, it wasn't like Mama's touch or Papa's and it wasn't really much help to the six-year-old.

"Shh, Betty, don't cry," she said softly. "It will be better tomorrow. Please don't cry." Betty continued to sob softly as she leaned into Cecile. As she spoke to Betty, her voice choked up as well and she began to cry, too. They were two delicate little girls locked up in a newly designated prison hospital. The events of the past day and the fear of the unknown as well as the madness all around were crushing to them. The cold, sterile room they were locked in had become their prison cell. However, lost in the unfolding tragedy was one of the greatest ironies of all.

This was the same hospital that both Cecile and Betty were born in.

Chapter Four

The girls were still sleeping when the door to their room opened. A guard and two nurses came in and the guard yelled at them to get up. The nurses each carried a basin and the guard pulled a cart with bottles on it.

"Up children. Up children," one of the nurses said.

Cecile awoke from her sleep to see the guard and the nurses and sprang up in fear.

"Don't worry, we are going to wash you," the nurse said.

Cecile woke Betty up. She was confused by the people in her room.

"Betty, it's time to get washed."

The younger girl wiped her eyes and looked at nurse. "Can we have breakfast now?"

"First we wash you. Then you can have breakfast."

The nurses undressed both girls. Cecile didn't want the nurse to take away her dress. She was afraid they would take it and she would lose her little doll.

"It will be right here on the side," the nurse said as she laid the dress down.

They washed both girls from head to toe. They were gentle with them. The water was warm and felt good. They were so caked with dirt and dust from the past several days and it was the first time they would wash in days.

When they were done being bathed, Cecile wanted to get dressed.

"Not yet," said the nurse. She went to the cart and got a scissors.

"What are you going to do?" Cecile cried.

The nurse would not answer.

"Please tell me. What are you doing?"

The nurse pulled a wriggling Cecile over to her. "I have to cut your hair and I don't want you to fight me. Now stay still."

A second nurse held Betty by the shoulders. She pulled a pair of scissors from her pocket as well.

"I don't want you to cut my hair. I don't want you to." Betty's frightened and pleading eyes were unable to stop the nurse.

"You have to be quiet. This must be done."

Cecile and Betty both struggled to avoid the cutting. But it was to no avail. The nurses had a job to do and soon the room was filled equally with the sounds of crying and the sound of scissors flashing. Within seconds, clumps of honey brown and blond hair fell to the cement floor of the room. Some fell into the sisters' laps, some stuck to the tears on their faces. But it didn't take long. The hair was gone, their princess locks were lying on the ground.

But it didn't stop with the haircuts. One of the nurses opened the largest of the bottles and the stench of kerosene quickly filled the room. Using sponges, the nurses washed each girl's hair with the kerosene, making sure there would be no presence of lice. It smelled so bad that Betty began to choke. But the nurses didn't stop. They scrubbed and scrubbed for minutes. There was virtually no hair left on their heads so the kerosene was absorbed directly by their scalps. Both girls cried out in pain.

When it was over, the nurses told the girls to get dressed. Both Betty and Cecile obeyed quickly.

"We'll bring you breakfast now. Then, maybe we'll let you walk around a little." The nurses left the room and slammed the door shut behind them. There was no sound except the sniffling of the girls as each looked at their hair lying on the ground of their cell.

The nurse shortly returned with two trays of food. There were plates and napkins and silverware, which the girls hadn't seen in many days. As bad as they felt, they energetically ate their breakfast, their first nourishment in quite a while, and each was hoping someone would bring another tray so they could eat some more.

A few hours later, the nurse who brought them breakfast told them they would be allowed to walk around the grounds. The girls went with the nurse and walked outside. No one yelled at them and no one called them names. Betty held onto Cecile's hand tightly as they walked and watched the others who were on the grounds.

"Do you know which room our Mama is in?" Cecile asked the nurse.

"Why yes, it's that one over there," she said, pointing to a room heavily protected with bars.

"Look Betty, that's Mama's room. That's where Mama is getting better."

"Can we see her?" Betty asked.

"I'm afraid not," the nurse said. "She's very sick and needs her rest. You won't be able to see her for a while."

Cecile felt some relief from knowing where her mother was. At least she could see the window and imagine her Mama resting peacefully and getting better every minute.

Many days went by as the little girls were forced to remain at the hospital. They were locked in their room for hours at a time and were only allowed out for a walk in the afternoon. They waited all day for the time the nurse would come and let them out. It was so much better than watching the courtyard from the window, which Cecile did for hours on end.

The nurses had come to know the girls and feel sorry for

them. One nurse gave Cecile a matchbox which she used to make a little toy bed for Betty. She used some wool from the blanket to make a little doll for her as well. Both girls then had dolls to play with. Cecile used whatever she could find to make other items for Betty to play with.

But the days went by slowly. They were, after all, just little children with absolutely nothing to do. All too often, they were left only with their thoughts of Papa and Marguerite and they cried for them. Cecile could not lose the site of the stadium as they pulled away in the ambulance and it haunted her all the time. The nights were the worst and neither girl was able to sleep very well. They desperately missed the love and security of their family. Sometimes Cecile would cry and sometimes it was Betty's turn. They each tried to make the other feel better as best they could.

On occasion, the nurses and guards would let Cecile and Betty wander the grounds with no supervision. The first time they did, they immediately ran to the window where Laja was recovering. A guard came over and told them they were not allowed to talk to their mother.

"Can't we say good morning to our Mama?" Cecile begged.

"No, absolutely not. You are not to say anything to her."

The girls missed Laja so much. They would sit on the grass beneath her window and just watch the bar- covered glass. They would make themselves see Laja's face, even though concrete and glass separated them. On one of the visits Cecile started to sing at the window. She sang one song and then another. Nobody stopped her. Betty joined in and both girls just sang and sang. They sang every song they knew and then started over and sang them all again.

"Do you think Mama heard us?" Betty asked

The window was shut tightly.

"I'm sure she did," Cecile said, but she was smart enough to realize that the closed window blocked the sound from the outside. Cecile knew they were singing for themselves. Soon, the nurse came over to them to take them back to their room.

The next day, they went to her window again. But this time, the window was open—not a lot but just enough. Cecile was thrilled when she saw the opening. This time, she knew Mama would hear her.

Cecile was right. From inside her room, Laja could hear the girls' voices. It was her first contact with them in many many days. She couldn't see them or touch them but she knew they were there and could hear for herself that they were all right. Tears of joy streamed down Laja's cheeks as she listened to the sweet sounds of her little girls' voices. The tears turned bitter-sweet though, as she thought of her other daughter and her husband. She had no idea where they were or if they were dead or alive.

Some of the guards who were French would actually ask the nurses to bring the children to the window to sing. They said it made Laja happy and as a result, she was getting better and better each day. But the French guards were themselves moved by the sounds of singing in their language. It reminded them of different times, when voices were raised in song by a proud people. Those days were long gone now as the Nazi noose was closing ever more tightly around the necks of every person living in France. Hearing the voices of the little girls took the guards away from their own pain, if just for a little while.

Still, every night was miserable for the Widermans. Cecile began to write messages on scraps of paper the nurses gave her to anyone who she thought could come and rescue them. She wrote mostly to her grandparents who lived in Paris. She had no idea if they were still in the city. She didn't see them at the truck depot or at the stadium. Did the Nazis take them away, too? Cecile and Betty talked about them all the time. It was easier to talk about them than about Papa and Marguerite. Sadly, none of her messages, written in the form of letters, were allowed to be sent.

One day, as the nurse was getting the girls their breakfast, she left the door open. Cecile peered out into the hallway in curiosity. She had gotten used to the room and the surroundings but liked to watch the business of the hospital, especially when no one knew she was watching.

A woman walked by the door in search of a patient she came to visit. It was the first person Cecile had seen who was not a guard or a nurse. It was just a person, coming to see a relative or a friend. Cecile watched her walking around, peering into each room. She quickly ran back to the bed and took a piece of paper and wrote her grandparents name and address along with her name, Betty's and Laja's.

"Excuse me," Cecile whispered when the woman walked by.

The woman looked at Cecile, startled to hear and see a child on that floor.

"What do you want, sweetheart."

"Could you please find my grandparents and tell them we are here. Their address is on this piece of paper."

"I can't do that," the woman said. "I could be in trouble for doing that. You are Jewish, right?"

Cecile didn't answer but just stared at the woman, her eyes wide open, pleading silently with the woman to help her. The visitor took the paper and stuffed it in her pocket.

"I'm sorry. I can't do that for you. If anyone finds out, my family will be the ones in trouble. I'm not even Jewish."

The woman looked around to see if anyone had seen her talking to Cecile. The hallways was quiet and no one had seen them.

"I would love to help you, but I can't. I'm sorry." The woman hurriedly walked down the corridor and down the stairs.

Cecile rushed back into the room and over to the window. She watched the woman disappear into the courtyard. She put her head into her hands and began to cry. They were alone, she thought. No one will ever help them. But the sadness disappeared and she soon shuddered with fear. "What if the woman would tell the Nazis where her grandparents lived?" "What if they weren't taken away yet and now, because she gave them the address, they would be caught and taken?" Cecile felt a sense of panic and was quiet for the remainder of the day.

Shortly after lunch the next day, the door opened and the nurse came in, along with a guard. Cecile and Betty had gotten used to the routine of taking their walks outside—after all, they had been there for a month now. But having a guard there was not part of the routine. Both the nurse and the guard had smiles on their faces and the girls were not afraid.

"We have a surprise for you," the nurse said.

"A surprise? What surprise?"

"Today, we are taking you to see your Mama. We can take you to her room."

"Mama, Mama" Betty began crying out. "I want to see my Mama!"

"You can," the nurse said. "But only for five minutes. Mama is feeling better and the guard will let you in for a little bit. But you must promise to be good and to leave when we tell you."

"We promise, we promise" both girls said, jumping up and down in their joy.

They ran down the hall filled with excitement, passing the stairway they usually walked down. Today they wouldn't go down those stairs. Today, they would see their Mama.

They got to their Mama's room and watched carefully as the guard took his keys out. The girls couldn't believe this was happening. They each felt like they hadn't seen her in months. They could think about her, sing to her, but now they were going to see her.

It seemed like hours were passing as the guard fumbled to open the door. When he did and the door flew open, Cecile and Betty rushed passed him to where Laja was lying in her bed.

"Mama, oh Mama. We missed you so," Cecile said, throwing herself onto her mother.

Betty was right behind her.

"Mama, we love you."

Laja burst into tears as the girls struggled to get closer to her. She was so frail and her skin was so pale but as she held her girls tightly, her blue eyes shone as if she was seeing heaven for the first time.

The three of them cried together as they clung to each other. The guard and the nurse quietly left the room out of respect for the three people who had been through so much already.

"Don't cry Cecile," Laja said. "Don't cry Betty. I'm here."

There was no stopping the girls. A month's agony spilled out of them.

"We missed you so much. We thought you were going to die. We thought we would never see you again," Cecile cried.

"No, no. You needn't worry about me. I'm so much better. Please, stop your crying." She looked straight at Betty and smiled at her. "Stop your crying now, my darling."

"We sang to you Mama. Every day. Did you hear us?" Cecile asked.

"Oh yes, I heard you every day. I looked forward to hearing you. I sometimes even sang along with you."

"I sang too," Betty said. "Did you hear me, too?"

"Of course. How could I not hear your beautiful voice."

"Can we stay with you Mama? Can we leave here today?" Cecile pressed herself tightly against her mother.

"Cecile, I have to speak to you," Laja said. There was a change in her tone. "I want to give you something and I want to talk to you."

Laja shifted to get her hands free. When she did, she slowly took off her wedding ring. Her fingers were so small and thin that the ring came off easily.

"I want you to hold my ring. I want you to hold it for a while, my darling. My fingers are so thin, it sometimes comes off. So you must take and hold it until it will fit me again."

"Alright Mama, but are we going home?"

"No darling, we're not. I don't know when we are going home. But I want you to do something for me. No matter what happens, I want you to take care of your sister and take care of yourself. Always. Think about Betty and yourself first. Do you hear me?"

"Yes, Mama, but what about you? You'll take care of us."

" I hope so. But in case I can't, I want you to know that I will always count on you. Whatever happens in this country, you and Betty are the most important people. You must always think only about each other and about getting away. I don't want you to think or worry about me, or Papa or Marguerite." She struggled to keep talking without breaking down in tears. It was too important.

"I will always think of you. I will always love my little girls and I want to know you will always take care of each other, even if I can't do it for you. I want to know you will always hold your sister's hand—wherever you go. Will you do that for me, Cecile?"

"Yes Mama, but you'll be with us."

"I hope so. Will you do that for me Betty? Will you take care of Cecile?"

"Yes Mama," the smaller voice said. "We'll take care of you too."

"Good." She held her daughters tightly for a few minutes, none of them speaking. They just drank each other in, touching, holding, being touched and being held.

The door opened and the nurse and the guard came back in.

"We have to go now," the nurse said. The Widermans didn't want to let go of each other.

The nurse pulled Cecile away from Laja, while the guard released the grip Betty had. Both girls were desperate in their tears. So was Laja.

"I love you both," Laja whispered. "Cecile, always hold your sister's hand. Remember that."

"We love you, Mama. We love you. We'll take care of you.

Don't leave us." Cecile turned to the guard. " Please we want to stay with Mama. Please."

But it didn't help. The nurse and the guard took the girls to the door. They let them have one more look at the frail and white Laja. Let them say I love you once more to each other and then turned and shut the door. They took the girls back to their room where they cried for the rest of the day and night.

Two days passed before the girls were relaxed again. As wonderful as it was to see their Mama, it was heartbreaking for them. All Betty spoke about was going back and seeing her again. Cecile had an uneasy feeling that that wasn't going to happen anytime soon.

A short time later a guard came to the room, all by himself. No nurse, just the guard.

"Come with me, girls," he said. They started to leave the room, but he turned back to Cecile. "Bring your doll with you."

Cecile didn't understand why but she had learned to do exactly what the guards said, when they said it. She scooped up her doll and put it back in her pocket.

They walked down another hallway, one they hadn't seen before. This time there were offices, not hospital rooms. They came to the last one in the hallway and he opened the door. The girls were shocked to look in and see their grandparents and their aunt standing by the window. Their father's parents had found them.

"Cecile, Betty, my darlings," she said in Yiddish. "We're so happy to see you," their grandmother said, bending down to catch the stunned girls, who had started running towards her. They kissed and hugged for a long time, their grandfather bent down to them as well.

"Girls, I have wonderful news for you," Grandfather said. "We are taking you home with us."

"You are?" Betty asked, amazed.

"Yes, right now!"

"To our house?" Cecile said.

"Sort of. We're all going to our house."

"Mama, too?" Cecile wanted to know.

"No darling, Mama is still too sick. She'll be coming soon. But you're leaving this hospital and coming home where you'll be safe."

"I want to stay near Mama," Betty protested.

"Oh no," her grandmother said sweetly. "You can't stay here anymore. There are too many sick people who are going to need your room to get well. And we need you to come back to our house and make it cheerful again."

Cecile had many emotions at once. She wanted to get out of the hospital so badly, she prayed for the moment they would leave and go back to life again—a life of family and other clothes and even school. But here she was faced with leaving without her Mama and she didn't much like that. Her grandmother was clear, though, that Mama couldn't go with them yet. She finally chose to believe her grandmother about Laja's eventual return, but she had her doubts.

Her grandfather spoke to the guards and the nurses about their leaving. There were papers to sign and instructions to be given. Her aunt had to act as an interpreter as her grandfather could only spoke Polish and Yiddish.

"Can I see my daughter?" Grandfather asked.

"No, we cannot let you do that."

"Why not? We are leaving and just want to see her for a moment."

"That is not possible. Sorry," he said coldly. But Grandfather stared at him for a long moment and the guard finally compromised. "I will let you leave the grounds near to where she is and allow you to wave to her." That was the best Grandfather was going to be able to get from the guard and he reluctantly agreed.

The five of them walked out of the office onto the grounds of the hospital that had been home for Cecile and Betty for more than a month. Both little girls were anxious to get beyond the gates but were sad to be leaving their Mama where she was.

They walked by the long row of hedges toward the hospital main gate. They stopped some 30 yards from a courtyard. Laja was sitting on a stoop along with several other women. Cecile, Betty, their aunt and their grandparents were frozen as they watched and waved to Laja. She seemed so beautiful in the distance.

Laja understood the girls were going free and tried to wave back but quickly brought her hand to her mouth, trying to hold back tears. The sight of her sitting there was too much for her children.

Cecile broke from her grandmother's hand and started to rush toward Laja. Her aunt caught her and held her. "No darling. You can't go. You heard what the guard said. She'll be home soon."

The emotions were hard on the Widermans, who could watch her from a distance, but couldn't touch her. They waved at Laja a little longer, but soon were escorted to the gate by the guards.

They had to go. They knew that. Herz's parents were afraid their mission to rescue their grandchildren might be stopped at any time. They knew they couldn't free Laja and they had no idea where their sons Robert and Herz were. At least they were lucky enough to get the children. They were worried sick for weeks about where the children were, until that woman came to their house and gave them Cecile's note. What an angel of mercy!

They were very near the gate of the hospital when Cecile stopped again. Her Mama was further away than before, but still in sight. Her aunt bent down to make sure she wouldn't try to run back into the courtyard. But Cecile wasn't running this time. Her shoulders dropped, her eyes watered and she simply blew her mother a kiss.

It was the last time she would see her mother, Laja Widerman.

Chapter five

What was left of the family left the hospital grounds very quickly. None of them, was sure they wouldn't be stopped and brought back so they left without looking back. It was the first time Cecile and Betty had been out of the hospital grounds in over a month and it looked to them that much had changed on the streets of Paris.

The hospital was not very far from where Cecile and Betty had lived, so within a short time, the streets began to look familiar to Cecile. She recognized some of the stores along the avenue, the school, a theater and the apartment buildings. In fact, she even saw where one of her friends lived. But there was something so strange about the streets in some of these neighborhoods of Paris. They were empty. There were no signs of life. Garbage was all over the ground, the stores were boarded up and there was absolutely no activity.

Even a child could understand what had happened. These were Jewish neighborhoods and the people who lived there had been taken away. While they didn't go through her own neighborhood, Cecile imagined it would look the same as the ones they passed. She pressed her nose against the car window as she watched the eerie, empty sight.

They finally got to their grandparents' apartment, which was very tiny, just two rooms. It was in a very bad part of the city, poor during the best of times. Now, during some of the worst times, it was even worse. Their father's parents had come to Paris from Poland to find a better life. For a while it was better. Grandfather was able to be a tailor, like he was in Poland and had a one room store near to where he lived. He was able to make ends meet and teach his granddaughter, Cecile, how to make clothes. Now, there were few city services. Garbage was piling up and very few people walked the streets.

Neither Betty or Cecile were too comfortable going up the stairs, the memory of the night they were taken away still burned inside them. If it could happen once, Cecile thought, then it could happen again. She tried to imagine why people in this neighborhood were not taken away. Were they going to be? If they were, would it be tonight? Tomorrow? Would they have to take that long walk to the truck depot again? Would they have to go to the stadium once more? And worse. What happened to the people once they left the stadium? Papa, Marguerite, Robert and Henri were at the stadium, but Cecile realized that whatever was going to happen to them had probably already happened.

So it was with great uneasiness that the girls walked through the front door of their grandparents' apartment. They were surprised to see their father's other sister and their cousin in the apartment. They lived in another part of the city, one that had been cleaned out by the Nazis a few weeks ago. They were lucky not to have been at home when they came, but now were forced to hide. If discovered, they would be taken away instantly by the Nazis.

"Welcome home, my darlings," Grandmother said when she locked the door behind her. "We are so happy to have found you and brought you back." She hugged each girl tightly. She was more affectionate than she had ever been.

But Cecile and Betty were tired. Their bodies were exhausted from a month of little sleep. Their minds were exhausted from fear and sadness. All they wanted to do was fall asleep. They kissed their aunt and cousin and sat down in a corner of the room.

Grandmother made food for them but they were too tired to eat.

"Cecile, Betty, why don't you have some supper?"

"I'm not hungry Grandmother. I would rather wait for breakfast," Cecile said.

"I'm not hungry either. I want to go to sleep."

Seven people in a tiny two room apartment. Grandmother tried to determine how they would all sleep.

"Betty and Cecile, why don't you two sleep in the bed with Grandfather and me?" Everyone else can find a place on the floor."

Cecile felt bad for her cousin. He was young, too. He had suffered over the past month just like they did. She wished there was another bed for him to sleep in.

The girls felt some sense of security due to the fact that there were so many of them. No strangers, all were people who knew them and loved them. They were used to seeing their aunts and cousins during holidays, or on special occasions, like Marguerite's engagement party. Now they were huddling together, trying to keep the madness all around them from getting inside.

Grandmother pulled the blankets down and Cecile and Betty climbed in. Cecile held her doll close as she lied in bed. She had gotten very used to making sure Betty was all right before she let herself fall asleep and tonight was no exception.

"Betty, when we get up tomorrow, let's sing for Mama again. Let's show Grandmother and Grandfather how we sang."

"I don't want to sing unless Mama can hear us," Betty said.

"Maybe she will. Maybe our singing will go all the way to the hospital."

"Alright Cecile. But I hope Mama can hear."

"Let's believe she will." Cecile huddled close to Betty and

gave her the doll to hold. In minutes the two little girls were fast asleep.

For several days, they stayed in the apartment. Grandfather went to the store to get some food. Once in a while, Grandmother went out as well. Everyone else, though, stayed inside. The girls' aunt and cousin were still being hunted by the Nazis and it was best that only those who had to be outside were outside.

As the days wore on, the girls' grandparents decided that they needed to create some kind of normal life for them. She asked around the neighborhood about what was happening in the schools in that part of the city. Was it safe for Jewish children to go to school? Could the teachers be trusted? Were there guards watching who came out of the apartments and into the streets?

Convinced all was manageable, Grandmother told the girls they would be returning to school. Cecile was happy to return. Betty was not. She was not ready to be separated from the family and sit in a classroom.

"I don't want to go back to school, Grandmother. I don't want to. They will hurt me."

"Oh, no they won't, Betty," Grandmother set out to convince her. "Everyone is there just to go to school, not to hurt anyone. School is the best place to be."

"If I don't like it, can I come home?" Betty asked.

"Well, I don't think you can come home, but I'm sure there will be nothing there you won't like."

"Can Cecile take me?"

"Of course! But she has to go to school too. She has to be on her own and so do you."

Reluctantly, Betty agreed to go back.

Grandmother found some clothes that would fit both girls and prepared to bring them to the new school. First, she had to explain some rules to them.

"If anyone asks you where you live, you can tell them you live here. But if anyone asks who you live with, just tell them your grandparents and one aunt. Tell them you don't know anything about any other of your relatives. Pretend you never saw your aunt and cousin. The bad men are looking for them and we don't want them to find them. Do you understand?"

"I understand," Cecile said.

"Me, too," Betty volunteered as well.

"I know you do my darlings. I know you will have fun going back to school."

Grandmother and Grandfather brought the children to school and registered them. They had much convincing to do in order for the school to allow them to attend and their daughter acted as interpreter once again. After all, they were Jewish and still had to wear their little yellow Stars of David pinned to their clothing. While Jews weren't strictly forbidden to go to school, expelling them or refusing to let them in wasn't exactly discouraged either.

Grandmother was very persuasive and the school agreed to let Cecile and Betty come in. Their grandparents dropped Cecile and Betty off at their classrooms and then left. They crossed their fingers that all would be well.

All was not going to be well.

There were few Jews attending the school. Many parents had simply pulled their children out of school. There was verbal abuse. There were fights and the sense of normalcy that many parents sought was no longer to be found in the classroom. It started quickly for the girls.

"Do we have to sit here with Jews?" one child asked the teacher.

"Yes, you do. We are not going to worry about that in this class," the teacher said, trying to cut off any potential problems early. "We are all here to learn."

"But we want Jews to die," another student said. "Look Jew, here's what we want for you," the boy said imitating a person being hung.

Other children began to chant "We hate Jews. We hate Jews." Soon, the majority of the class had joined in the chant. Some of them got up out of their seats so they could stand next to Cecile and shout in her ear. The teacher had all she could do to stop the class from taunting her in a further, more dangerous way.

At first, Cecile put up with the taunts. She heard them in the streets. She heard them in the stadium, in the ambulance, at the hospital and didn't want to let the other children get the best of her. But she was only 11 years old and before the day was out Cecile could take no more.

Several of the students had drawn Stars of David and cut them out. They put glue on the back of them and pasted them to Cecile's clothing. There were simply too many of them. She would not go to school if this was what was going to happen. As she sat in her chair and cried, the others just laughed harder and taunted her more. Even the teacher had stopped trying to help her.

Cecile got up and ran out of the classroom. She grabbed Betty from her class and ran out of the main door of the school out into the street. No one at the school even tried to stop them.

When they got back to their grandparents house, they were quite upset. Grandfather was surprised to see the girls home so soon and saw that something had happened to them.

"What happened girls? Why are you home so soon?"

"It was horrible," Cecile blurted out. "I'm never going back again."

"Come here darling," her grandfather said. "Tell me why you're upset."

"Grandfather, they hate me," Cecile said. "I did nothing to any of them and they hate me. They put things on me, they called me names and they said they hoped I would die. What did I ever do to any of them? I never hurt them. Why do they want to hurt me?"

Grandfather tried to explain to the children what was happening in Paris. It wasn't easy. Life had changed relatively quickly for Jews in France and it was hardest for the children to understand why.

"They hate you because the Nazis are convincing people that Jews are bad. Everyone has a little bit of hate inside them and the Nazis are helping people to bring it out. They are blaming the Jews for everything that is bad in Paris, in France and in the world. We know it's not true, and so do most people, but everyone is so afraid for themselves that they listen to the Nazis telling them who to hate. We Jews happen to be the ones they are hating now. Tomorrow it might be Catholics, certainly Blacks and anyone else they feel can be the target. We just have to be patient and ride it out."

"Well, I'm not going back to school until the hating is over," Cecile said convincingly.

"I'm not going back to school either," Betty added, crossing her arms in defiance.

"Alright, alright, maybe going back to school isn't the best thing right now."

Later that night, as the girls were getting ready for bed, Betty asked Grandmother where her father and sister were.

"When am I going to see my Papa again?" she asked.

Grandmother took a great sigh and sat on the corner of the bed. She wanted to protect her granddaughters from the cold truth. It was likely that they would never see their Papa again. But as much as the old woman felt Herz, and Marguerite for that matter, were gone forever, she wanted the girls to hold out hope they were all right and keep trying to find them, at least until they could find out the truth. The girls had lost their father, but she had lost her two sons. Somewhere there must be answers.

"Betty, the Nazis have taken your father and sister away. We don't know where they took them. Maybe to the forest to cut down more trees, maybe to a hospital like Mama. But no one has told us where they are. You can be sure of one thing, though, wherever they are, they want to be back here with you."

"Are they dead?" Cecile asked. This was the first time Cecile posed the horrible question.

"We can't think of that, darling," Grandmother said. "We must try to believe they are both all right and will soon be coming back for us."

"I am afraid they are never coming back," Cecile said as she started to cry.

"Oh, come now, little one. Please don't cry. Wherever they are, Papa and Marguerite would not want you to cry for them. They would want you to be strong for you and your sister. You must try not to cry anymore. Even Mama in the hospital would want you to have dry eyes. Try not to cry—try for them. Will you do that?"

"I don't know, Grandmother. I miss them so much. It hurts to miss them so much."

"It hurts all of us, but we're all going to try. If we cry, the Nazis will know who we are. We can't let that happen, can we?"

"No Grandmother," Cecile said, growing very quiet in her sadness.

Cecile went into bed. Her cousin and her aunt were sleeping on the floor near the front door. Her other aunt was sleeping on the floor on the other side of the room. Grandfather was in bed, so was Betty. It was just Grandmother and Cecile left awake.

"I love you Grandmother," Cecile said as she held the old woman around the back of her neck.

"I love you too Cecile," Grandmother shuddered from her own tears as she held her granddaughter.

"I thought we weren't going to cry?" Cecile said.

"I'm not crying, darling. I'm not crying. We can't let them see us cry."

Cecile and Betty stayed in the house for days and days. The family amused themselves by playing games or reading. Sometimes they went out for a while, but it was becoming more dangerous. There were many rumors about regarding what was happening in the streets. More Jews being taken away. Many were shot in the street. Stories of Jews being beaten had become so frequent, they were seen as an everyday part of life.

The most disturbing stories were the ones Grandmother and Grandfather had been hearing when they left the house, but had kept to themselves. There were stories of people being taken away to slave camps where they were worked until they died. Not the kind of camp where Herz had cut trees, but cruel places, where guards shot those who didn't work hard enough or fast enough. Cruel places where mothers were separated from their babies and used to make Nazi babies. Cruel places where there was virtually no food and hundreds of people died every day. They were places where they were sending Jews taken right from their homes. It was probably the destination of all those in the stadium and from the empty neighborhoods around Paris.

The grandparents didn't share these rumors with the younger ones. They felt little need to subject them to the fear that came along with knowing these stories. But they did feel the noose tightening around their necks.

A woman from the building knocked on the front door. The children were in the back room. Grandfather stayed quiet, as he always did until the person identified himself. But the knocking kept up. Finally Grandfather walked over and asked who it was. The neighbor identified herself. Grandfather opened the door.

"Please," the woman said. "Make sure the children stay in the other room."

"Good God, why?" Grandfather said.

"I must tell you something. They shouldn't hear. Please."

"Alright, they'll stay in the back. What is it?"

"They are coming. They are coming to this neighborhood. I heard from my sister that they have begun to round Jews up again. They have started on the east side and will no doubt be here in a few days. Already there are more guards on the street. They are coming!"

"Calm down, please. I don't want everyone to panic," Grandfather said.

"We'll have to do something tomorrow," Grandmother added.

"What can we do? What can we do?" the woman said in a high pitched, frightened voice.

"The first thing is not to get excited," Grandfather said. "We have to think clearly and determine the best ways to hide. Thank you for the warning. We appreciate it. Tomorrow we must act without anyone realizing it. Please, it's time we went about our business."

The woman was surprised by Grandfather's calm. It seemed to help her too. She was much younger than Grandfather and looked to him in a fatherly way. She took a deep breath, stood up and left the apartment.

There was silence in the room for a few minutes after the neighbor left.

"The time is coming. I would like to ask Memere to take Cecile and Betty for a while," Grandmother said.

"You are probably right," her husband said.

Memere, whose real name was Lucie Boisgontier, was a friend of the girls' grandparents. A Catholic, she lived in Normandy with her husband Georges, and already was caring for several Jewish children. She had a tiny stone house in the small town near the English Channel and had been friends with Grandmother for many years.

Two days later, while Cecile and Betty were playing in the apartment, Grandfather came in with Memere.

"Children, I would like you to meet someone. This is Memere."

"Hello children," Memere said. "How are you today?" She had a pleasant sounding voice which matched perfectly with her round smiling face and very rotund body. She was very short, too, which made her seem less intimidating to the children than other adults they had encountered recently.

"We're fine," Cecile said.

"What a nice doll," she said to Cecile, who had the doll nearby as she always did.

"I got it for my birthday."

"Oh, very nice. How old are you?"

"I'm 11," Cecile said.

"I'm six," Betty added."

"Those are very nice ages for such pretty girls like you."

"Cecile, Betty, Memere is going to take you for a little vacation. She lives in a house near the ocean! You've never seen the ocean but it's very beautiful and you'll be able to go to school, go outside and play and be little children again," Grandfather said.

"I don't want to go on a vacation. I would rather stay here," Cecile said.

"Well, my darling. I don't think its very good to stay here any longer. I wouldn't want the bad men to come and find you. Do you?"

"No. But won't they find you and grandmother and everyone else?"

"I don't think so, but I think we all need to go away from Paris so they don't find us." Grandfather had no intention of leaving the city but having Cecile and Betty believe they did would make them more willing to go.

"There are children to play with and when all is quiet here again you can return," Memere said to the girls.

"But you should leave this morning. Don't you think so, Memere?"

"Oh yes, the sooner the better."

Grandfather gave Memere a bag that had money inside. It was money to be used to care for Cecile and Betty. It was a small price to pay to this woman, who was risking her life for the sake of the children. If the Nazis found she was hiding Jews, she would be executed. Memere didn't worry about the risk. Saving as many children as she could was most important to her.

Grandmother came out from the back room with a satchel with some clothes for the children.

"Cecile, Betty, it's best that you go with Memere. I wouldn't let you go if it wasn't good for you. You're the most important people to us right now and making sure you'll be safe with Memere is the best thing I can do for you. Your Mama would want you to go with Memere too."

"Will Mama know where we are?" Cecile asked.

"We will tell her as soon as we see her."

"I think it's time that we be going," Memere said.

Grandmother picked up Cecile and held her tight. She sat down and let Betty come to her too. Grandfather also hugged the girls. They both knew they were sending the girls away forever. They hoped and prayed they were doing the right thing.

"We love both of you, we always will," the old man said. "When it is safe we'll be together again."

"You promise?" Cecile asked.

"I promise," he said with voice cracking.

Memere took each girl by the hand and moved to the door. As she opened it, Cecile turned around and ran back into her grandparents' arms. She wouldn't let go for a long minute.

"Be brave, take care of your sister and don't cry," Grandfather said.

"I will, Grandfather. I will. I love you."

"I love you too, darling."

Slowly, they walked through the door and down the hall. Once in the street, Memere took the girls to the train station in the hope of boarding a train for Normandy. They were three French citizens and if no one saw them, they could get out of Paris.

Grandfather had given them the best chance they would have to survive the madness that had engulfed the country and the whole world. There were several underground organizations working throughout France, as well as in other countries, that would aid refugees on the run. Grandfather had known a man from one of these organizations, Ouvre de Secoure Aux Enfants, which is loosely translated as People Helping Children. Once he had contacted Memere and arranged for her to take the children, he then spoke to the man from O.S.E. and asked him to look in on the girls when they were in Memere's care. He told Grandfather not to worry. He said they would.

Luck was with Memere and the girls and within two hours they were on their way out of Paris toward the coast. They would start a new life—a life of hiding, a life of cunning and a life requiring steel nerves. From that moment on, Cecile and Betty would only survive if they were lucky. They had now become hidden children. They were on their own. Memere needed luck as well. Her life hung in the balance, too.

Several years later, Cecile and Betty would find out the Nazis stormed the neighborhood and their grandparents were taken away that very night.

Chapter Six

The two little girls stared at the countryside moving by them. Once they passed through the city it all looked different. There were farms, fields and tiny houses spread out sometimes with miles between them. It seemed so foreign to Cecile and Betty but at the same time, they were comforted by the scene. No city buildings, no rushing through the streets and best of all, no signs of Nazis.

Still, Cecile held Betty's hand very tightly. She remembered what her mother said—hold Betty's hand and never let go. As long as they were holding each other's hand, nothing would happen to them. No matter how Betty shifted in the seat, the two still were sitting hand in hand.

"Are we going to a farm?" Cecile finally asked Memere, who was watching the girls watch the countryside.

"We don't live on a farm, my darling, but there are many farms near us. Our house is very near the beach. In fact, from the beach near the house, you can almost see the whole world."

"Are there any Nazis there?"

"Not like in Paris, Cecile," Memere said softly. "There are some soldiers, but not all around you like in the city."

"Do they know we are Jewish?"

"No. They don't know you are Jewish and you must never tell them. You must never tell anyone."

"Will they take us away if they find out we are Jewish?"

"They might, darling. That's why we must never tell them."

"I won't tell them. Memere."

"That would be best."

"How many other children are there, Memere?" Cecile asked.

"We have six children. You will be our seventh and eighth. And we have a dog and eight cats."

"A dog and eight cats! Can I feed them and play with them?"

"Of course you can, darling. And you can too, Betty."

At each station, there were soldiers to be seen. They were watching the train go by, watching the people getting on and getting off. Cecile's heart raced every time they got near a station. She was frightened of the way they stared, the way they held their rifles and the way they stopped some people who just seemed to be walking on the platforms.

Memere watched carefully at each station too. She was taking a dangerous chance being with these children. If they were found to be Jews, it would mean death to all of them. But what could she do? She had to take the chance. These little ones had no chance if she or someone like her didn't watch over them.

This was the seventh time Memere had rescued Jewish children and brought them to her house. It was always close. It was always frightening. She knew that each of the children she had taken would become orphans very soon after they went with her and she believed these innocent youngsters were the greatest victims of what was happening in France and in other parts of Europe.

She breathed a sigh of relief every time the train pulled out of a station. They were safe, at least until they got to the next station.

There was a great commotion when they pulled into Caen. It was bigger than the other stations. The buildings around the station were also larger and there was a greater sense of the German occupation than at the other, smaller stops.

When the train stopped, a dozen soldiers jumped on board near the front car. There was a lot of activity on the platform and in a few minutes, the soldiers came off with five people, four men and a woman. They looked older than Marguerite and Henri, Cecile thought, but not too much older. Not like her parents. Their heads were down and they were carrying small bags. The soldiers had their guns pointed at them and they were pushing them on the platform. Two men in black coats came over and stood talking to them for a long while. Cecile could only imagine what they were saying.

After a while, the soldiers took the people into the station and then waved at the train to start moving. Memere and the girls let out brief sighs as the wheels clanked against the tracks. As they passed the station, they could see the five people being pushed and hit by the soldiers. They could have been anyone. They could have been Jews, they could have been members of the French resistance, they even could have been common criminals. But whoever they were, Memere knew they were done and the girls were reminded once again what the Nazi soldiers would do to people and all the pleasant farms and fields they would pass couldn't make them relax.

"Cecile," Memere said compassionately to the youngster who had grown silent since the station. "You must never let anyone know you are Jewish."

"I know, Memere," Cecile said without looking at her. "I won't tell anyone."

As they got near the coast, they could see the water from both sides. The girls had never been to the ocean and they watched intently. They imagined what was on the other side of the water. Did it look like France? Were the people friendly? Were the Nazis there too?

"Cecile, Betty, we will soon be at the station. It's time to get ready to go," Memere said. She could see fear instantly fill the girls faces and she was as calm as she could be. If all was well, there would be no one at the station and they would be able to get off easily. If there were soldiers when they got off, they would have to pass them and perhaps they would be stopped. Memere hoped against hope the girls' fear would not give them away.

The train pulled into the small station at Normandy without fanfare. There was a single guard at the back end of the platform but he didn't appear to be in any rush to watch who got on or off. After a four hour train ride, they were far enough away from Paris to find things different. There was no sense of panic like there was in the city. Normandy was a sleepy little community and all who were there were content to keep it so.

"Cecile, Betty, when we leave the train, hold my hand and we'll walk through the station. There doesn't seem to be anyone there and we are just returning home."

When Memere and the girls stood up, Memere tried to put one girl on each side of her. Cecile wouldn't let her. She had to hold Betty's hand herself. She had promised her mother and she wouldn't break her promise, no matter what.

They left the train and they could feel the steam coming from underneath the black locomotive. The single soldier was far away and they walked out of the station without incident. Both girls were very frightened but did nothing to give themselves away. They simply walked out of the station.

There was no car waiting for them and no taxis or buses to take them were they were going. They had to walk. Hand in hand they walked through the French countryside. Sometimes Memere would ask them to sing. Sometimes they walked along in silence. But no matter what they did, Cecile held Betty snugly by the hand and would not stop thinking about her parents, her sister, her grandparents and the others who were now very far away from them and in so much danger.

Memere's house was five miles from the station and the

walk took over two hours. They were all quite tired and both of the girls asked over and over again if they were going to be there soon. It was not like the walk to the depot when the Nazis first came to their house, but it felt every bit as long.

Cecile was amazed at the smell of the ocean and the kinds of flowers that were growing on the side of the small road. Betty said nothing but from time to time let out a whimper, half from exhaustion, half from bewilderment. However, neither girl complained and neither did anything to make the walk more difficult.

After a long time had passed and the conversation and songs had ended, Memere pointed way up the road.

"That is our house. That's where I live."

"I am hungry," Betty said. "I am so tired too."

"Don't worry darling. Soon you will have supper and be able to go to sleep."

Memere lived in a tiny stone house. It looked quite weather-beaten and old but from a distance, Cecile was able to see light coming from inside and smoke sputtering up the fireplace. It made her feel more relaxed.

Memere walked inside the small house. It had only two rooms and with the six children, the animals and her husband, it was full of activity.

"We're home," Memere said pleasantly as she walked in. She saw her husband Georges and gave him a nod which said everything was fine. He smiled at her and then at the children, standing hand in hand in the doorway.

"Come in children," Georges said. "Welcome home. You must be hungry and tired from your trip."

Cecile and Betty slowly walked in and looked around. Memere held Cecile by the hand, bent down to one knee and introduced them to her husband.

"Cecile, Betty, this is my husband, Georges. Everyone here calls him Pepere. You can too."

"Hello Cecile," Pepere said. "How are you. It's very nice to meet you."

Cecile shook his hand tentatively. So did Betty. Georges Bosgointier was a gruff looking man, very thin and a little withdrawn, without the twinkle in the eye their Papa had. Neither girl knew if they were going to like him. But still, he spoke kindly to them and for the moment, that was enough.

A small dog jumped on Cecile and it made her smile. She petted him and called him a good dog. She almost laughed. Betty wanted to pet the dog and he jumped up and was able to lick the younger girl on the face. She mimicked her sister and called him a good dog, too.

The six other children looked at the girls as warily as Cecile and Betty looked at them. Each one had a tragic, heartbreaking story to match the newcomers. Each had been rescued by Memere, some after they had already been taken.

The youngest of the children, Rene, was the child of a French woman who had been brutally raped by the Nazis. Memere took him as her own.

The others, young boys named Maurice, Bernard and David, Sami and Jacquot had been taken, one at a time, from the arms of Jewish woman who had begged Memere to save them. Memere took two of the children from their mothers who were actually being guarded by soldiers. When they turned to quiet another prisoner, Memere took the children and simply walked out of the detention area.

The others came as Cecile and Betty did, from desperate Jews who knew they were about to be taken by the Nazis and couldn't bear what would happen to them. The worst thing about the deportations was the helplessness with which parents were forced to live. When a parent can no longer protect a child, life has been reduced to a hell on Earth. With desperate words, desperate eyes and all the money they had left, they pleaded with Memere to find safety for their children. They knew they would likely be killed and the thought of their innocent children suffering the same fate was too much to bear and they begged this small, round French citizen with the kind face to save them. Memere could not resist helping them.

Pepere was not happy about the risk. But he wasn't there for the begging or the pleading. If he was, he would not likely be able to walk away either. He reluctantly agreed each time Memere came home with another child. No one deserved what these children had waiting for them. As much as he feared what would happen to all of them if they were caught, Pepere was willing to make each child part of the family and would at least be kind to them.

Still, it was Memere who took the greatest risk. She walked into the dungeons and pulled off the rescues. She could have been shot on the spot. Memere, and people like her, faced the darkest side of humanity and with compassion and bravery saved thousands of young lives.

Betty and Cecile, along with the others, had dinner. The others were used to each other and spoke and even laughed as they ate. They even tried to bring the newcomers into their conversation and little table games. Cecile and her sister were not quite ready for the family fun taking place at the table. They sat quietly.

"Betty and Cecile," Memere said. "We are all safe here in Normandy. No one knows any of you are here and no one bad will come to look for you. When your parents are able, they will know where to find you. Please try to relax and try to enjoy yourselves." Memere lied. She knew that each of their parents were probably already dead or would be very soon. There would be no coming back for these children.

After dinner, Memere and Pepere arranged for the children to go to sleep. The two rooms had little beds scattered all around. When Memere put down two blankets for Cecile and Betty to go to sleep in, the girls refused to climb in alone.

"Betty will sleep with me, Memere," Cecile said.

"You might be more comfortable in your own bed, darling," she said.

"No, I want to sleep with Cecile," Betty said.

"That's all right, you can sleep with your sister."

Betty climbed in next to Cecile. She held the little girl tightly and whispered for her to go to sleep. It had been a long day and just this morning, they had been with their grandparents. They had been through so much already. Cecile couldn't understand why any of this was happening.

"Why do they hate Jews?" she asked herself. "Why do they want to kill us? Why did they take my Papa and Mama and sister away? When will they come to get us?"

She cried herself to sleep that night. She cried silently and to herself. After all, she had to take care of Betty like her Mama said and she didn't want Betty to see her crying. She might be frightened or hungry or sad but the well being of her little sister would always come first now. They were all each other had.

One by one the eight children fell asleep. Two were so sad that Memere had to sit by them and comfort them. Each time another child came into the "family," each child was reminded of the tragedy in their own lives. It was too much for some of the young ones to bear. Memere's dog fell asleep too. He would stay in each corner of the room for a while and then find a child to snuggle up with. He seemed to pass from child to child during the night, providing protection and security for them.

"Lucie, we cannot keep all these children," Georges said once it was quiet and all the children were sleeping.

"I know that Georges, but I couldn't say no to Betty and Cecile. They come from such a wonderful family and were facing tragedy at any moment. What could I do?"

"You did what you needed to, but now we are faced with a problem of what to do. Did these girls' grandparents give you any money?"

"Yes. They gave me money and a few things for them."

"I think we are going to have to have someone else care for them. We don't have any more room."

"I don't think we can separate these girls from anything else, Georges. They have been pulled apart from loved ones many times already. I don't know if they are strong enough to go through it again."

"We are going to have to. We have two rooms and eight children. We are two more so that means ten people in this place. Even eight is way too much. I think tomorrow we are going to have to find a place for them. I'm sure they are wonderful children but we simply have no room for them.

"You got them out of Paris and up to Normandy. That was difficult enough. But they're here, and if we can find them a home, they can stay here. If we don't find them a home, it will soon lead to questions and answers we don't have. We don't want to call attention to ourselves, do we? I know a farmer outside Normandy. I will speak to him tomorrow about Betty and Cecile. They'll be safe there and we'll be able to take these girls to them. Who knows, maybe they'll take even more and we can bring back some other children next time. We should speak to him before we become too attached to these two."

"I think it's too late, Georges. These two are already special. Do you see how Cecile looks after Betty? Do you see how Betty clings to her older sister? They have seen too much already."

"But you still know that I am right. We can make no mistakes or we'll be found out. When I see the farmer tomorrow, I will tell them they are the children of my widowed friend in Paris who has gone away for a while. He'll be sending for the youngsters very soon."

"Alright. But let's keep an eye on them. I don't want anything to happen to them," Memere reluctantly agreed.

"Good," Georges said. He was not a compassionate man and felt there was nothing else he could do that made any sense. He would take them tomorrow. They would be all right on the farm They might even like it. At least they'd like it more than a two room stone house with eight other people.

Memere fell asleep quickly. Pepere stared at the ceiling for a while. The gentle sound of the children's secure sleep was echoing all around him. It was musical. It put him to sleep as well.

In the morning, Pepere was out early. He went to see the farmer about Cecile and Betty. Memere made sure all the children were dressed and ate breakfast. The small kitchen area yielded little in the way of food but Memere was always sure that the children would at least eat something. Anything they could grow they ate. It was mostly a diet of soups, vegetables and the like. There was rarely any meat. Children, however, only knew their stomachs were empty and they eagerly ate whatever meals Memere could put together.

After breakfast Pepere returned. He nodded to Memere with a nod that said their plan was approved by the farmer. Memere and Pepere took Cecile and Betty outside.

"Cecile, Betty, my darlings. I want you to do something for me."

"What do want us to do, Memere?" Cecile asked.

"I want you and Betty to go and stay with a farmer friend of Pepere's. He and his wife live a few miles from here and while we try and make some more room here, we want you to stay with them. They have no children of their own and they are really excited that you will come to live with them, even for a while."

"I don't want to go to the farmer," Betty began to cry. "I want to stay here with you."

"Do we have to go away again, Memere? Please can we stay with you and Pepere and the other children," Cecile pleaded.

"My darlings," Memere bent down and held both girls. "If there are too many of us here, people will know and we will not be safe. You'll be safe at the farmer's house for a few weeks and then you'll come back."

Cecile dropped her eyes. She held Betty's hand very tightly. It was time to leave someone she had grown to trust once again. She was crying because she was afraid for her and Betty. She was crying because once again she was facing the unknown and the danger she knew was out there.

"We'll do whatever you say, Memere. My grandparents told me to do whatever you told us and we'll go."

Memere tried to hug Cecile to show her she wouldn't let her down, but Cecile wouldn't return her embrace. Once Memere let go, Cecile took Betty by the hand and walked toward the house.

"Betty, we have to get our things. We have to go to a new family for a while. I don't want you to be afraid, we will be together."

"Don't be sad Cecile," Betty tried to reassure her older sister. "Soon Papa and Mama will come for us and we'll go home again."

"I know they will, Betty. Don't you be sad either."

Cecile was having more and more doubts about ever being reunited with her family again.

Chapter Seven

The ride to the farmer's house was long, but it wasn't nearly as long as the other rides Betty and Cecile had taken recently. It was equally as unnerving. After all, they didn't know the farmer and, in fact, had never even been on a farm.

All the way on the road, Pepere had been watching the girls carefully. He wondered if they were doing the right thing. He hoped the farmer and his wife would care for them and prayed they would not be betrayed.

"Cecile," he said. "The farmer doesn't know you are Jewish. You must not tell him. You must only say your father has left to start a new life and will send for you when he is settled. Do you understand that?"

"Yes Pepere. I understand. We won't say a word."

Memere also impressed upon the girls how important it was not to let anyone know they were Jews.

"If they were to know you were Jews, it would be the end for all of us. You won't tell them now, will you?" she asked.

"I promise to never tell," Betty said. She held up her hand as if in a swear.

Cecile promised, too and then continued to watch the country-side disappear house by house right before her eyes. In one hand she held her sister's hand very tightly. In her other, she held her little bag of memories equally tight.

The farmhouse was old, but not unpleasant. Cecile and Betty could see a few cows in the field and stared intently at them. They had never seen cows before.

"Those are cows my darling. That's how we get milk," Memere explained.

"Will they eat us?" Betty wanted to know.

"No, no, Betty. They eat grass and then give you good, fresh milk. They are friendly and will not bother you."

There were chickens in the yard as well. The girls didn't know what they were for and Memere had to explain that to them as well. A dog slept by the front door and barely moved as Memere and Pepere brought them to the house.

The farmer's wife saw them coming and came to open the door.

"Here already? We tried to make some room for the little ones so they would be comfortable. We didn't know you would arrive so soon. Come in. Come in, please."

Pepere thanked the farmer's wife and they all entered the house.

Cecile examined the inside of the house. She thought how different it looked from her apartment in Paris. It even looked different from Memere's house. There was a lot of furniture but it all looked very old. It wasn't soft-looking like her grandparents furniture. Everything looked cold to Cecile. In fact, the only thing that seemed warm to her was the fire in the fireplace, which was sputtering in the corner.

The two girls just stood there as Pepere gave the woman a bag containing the money their grandparents had given Memere.

"This should be enough to take care of them," Pepere said. Cecile could see he was a little nervous as he handed her the bag.

"I'm sure this will be fine..for a while. If we need any more we'll let you know." The woman started counting the money right there in the front room.

"The girls will be no problem for you," Memere said to her.

"They are wonderful children and will be happy to work in the fields and do whatever chores need to be done here. I think you will enjoy having them as much as they will enjoy being here. Isn't that right, Cecile?"

"Yes Memere," Cecile said quietly. She was frightened.

"Yes Memere," Betty chimed in, too. She was more confused than anything else.

The silence that followed was broken by Memere. "I think it is time for us to be going. You have a lot of work to do and we have to be getting home." She could see by the way Cecile's eyes followed her that she didn't want them to leave.

"Girls, come outside with us and let me show you how nice it looks," Memere said. The girls followed her outside.

There were tears in Memere's eyes as she gave one last set of instructions to the girls her friends had place in her trust.

"Don't be frightened, darlings. It will be all right. In this life, we all must do some things we are afraid of. The time will pass and you will be fine. Just listen to the farmer and don't let them know who you really are. Do you understand?"

"Yes, Memere, we said we understand," Cecile said somewhat impatiently.

"No," Memere said emphatically. "Please, please, remember what we told you. If you make a mistake it could be the end of all of us. Do this for you, for us, your family and for other families like yours. You must learn to grow up now and you must learn what your responsibility is."

"I know what to do Memere. You don't have to worry about me. I know what to do." Memere was taken at how far beyond her years this little girl sounded.

Pepere and the farmer's wife came out of the door as Memere was hugging each child. He thanked her again and they prepared to leave.

"Don't forget to hold Betty's hand, Cecile," Memere said.

"I won't. Will you come to see us, Memere?"

"Yes, my darling. I will come to visit you soon."

"Good-bye for a little while, Betty," Memere bent down to the younger child.

"Good-bye for a little while, Memere."

Memere turned to the farmer's wife. "I'll come to see them soon. Thank you for caring for them in the meantime."

"Don't worry about them. There is plenty to do and they'll be all right."

Cecile and Betty watched Memere and Pepere walk down the road. Cecile couldn't help letting a sigh escape as she wondered what life with the farmers was going to be like. Betty waved to the couple as they disappeared down the road.

"Come in children. Let's get to know each other and I'll show you what we do here." They walked back into the farmhouse somewhat bewildered.

Over the course of the next few days, the girls were taught how to live on a farm. They were given chores to do and did them as best they could. Memere's words about hiding who and what they were rang true inside Cecile and she said very little. It was better to say nothing at all than to say something that might give them away.

For her part, Betty followed Cecile's lead and spoke as little as her sister.

During the days, the girls would pick apples and take care of the animals. They learned to work in the fields and to care for the equipment the farmer had.

The farmer and his wife were pleasant to the children but they lacked the warmth the girls were used to. They reminded the girls of the doctors and nurses at the hospital their Mama was in. They weren't mistreated, they weren't spoken to angrily, but there was a coldness to the farmer and his wife. At night, they would eat dinner, always a hearty meal, and bedtime would come soon after. The farmer had a radio and he and his wife would listen to music before bed. Cecile and Betty wouldn't listen to the news programs or other talking shows, but they appreciated the music.

They slept in a room that had been used for storage. The farmer's wife made them a comfortable bed in the corner and Betty and Cecile shared the bed, as usual. Each night Cecile would tell Betty a story about better days. Sometimes they recalled crawling into bed with their parents to sing songs. Other times they spoke about going to grandfather's tailor shop to help make clothes. They even spoke about Marguerite's pending wedding.

The stories of the past, shared quietly in bed, comforted the girls for a time, but always there was a sadness by the end and they had to hold each other very tightly to keep their fears and sadness from overcoming them.

One morning during breakfast there was a knock on the door. It was raining very hard and the farmer was in the barn feeding the animals. The farmer's wife answered the knock.

The door opened and there were two German soldiers standing there. Cecile froze as she saw them from the kitchen table. She could barely decide whether to bring the spoon up to her mouth or put it down in the cereal.

"Can I help you?" the farmer's wife said.

"Do you mind if we come in and dry off?" one of them said.

"No, come in. Would you like coffee? It's fresh."

"Thank you, I think we will." She went to the kitchen and poured coffee for the men. "You have a nice house here. It's comfortable."

"Thank you very much. We don't have much company."

"Where is your husband?"

"He's in the barn, tending to the animals. He should be in in a moment."

"Madam," the first German spoke, "we have had word that people have come from some of the cities like Paris, Versailles and Orleans to find refuge here. These people are criminals and we must find them. Many are Jews and as you know, Jews are to be identified to the authorities. You haven't seen any of these people, have you?"

"Jews? There are no Jews here. We haven't seen anyone who shouldn't be here," the farmer's wife said.

Cecile sat very still with her spoon in her hand and listened. Betty continued to toy with her food, too. She had seen German soldiers before and had learned first hand what they can mean to innocent people.

"I'm sure you haven't seen anyone, Madam," the other soldier said. "We are just here to remind you that if you do, you must come and tell us. We will take care of them at that point."

Cecile recalled the soldiers in her apartment, at the depot, the stadium, at the train station at Caen and tried to hold her breath. She dropped her spoon by accident. When all eyes turned to her, she just smiled. They went back to their discussion.

"We'll be sure to lock our doors at night and look for anything out of the ordinary."

"I'm sure you will. Strange people could be dangerous and we of course would not want anything to happen to French citizens. Just don't give the Jews or others any help and again, make sure you report it."

"You can be sure my husband and I will report anything we see."

"Well, thank you for the coffee. You are very kind, " the officer said. They stood up to leave. One of them looked straight at Cecile and Betty. The girls continued to sit frozen at the table.

"These are nice children, Madam. You must be very proud. I have three girls back home."

"Thank you very much. They are very helpful around the farm."

They put on their coats, thanked the farmer's wife again and disappeared out the door without saying another word.

Once they were gone, everyone was still. The farmer's wife had never had an encounter with soldiers before and she was frightened. Cecile and Betty had already had many encounters with German soldiers and were even more frightened. Cecile remembered what Memere warned her about.

"What did those men want?" Cecile asked.

"They were looking for bad people and looking for Jews. If we find any Jews we must report them. Do you understand that?"

"Oh yes," Cecile said. "We haven't seen any."

Cecile was shaking as she spoke. She put her hand down so the woman wouldn't see it but it was too late.

"Are you all right, Cecile?"

"Oh yes. I'm fine. The soldiers made me nervous."

"Don't be afraid. The only ones who need to be afraid are criminals and Jews. Since we are all French, they won't bother us."

Cecile couldn't make herself relax, no matter how she tried. She wasn't sure if the farmer's wife felt sorry for her or suspected her.

Memere came to visit a few days later. The girls were so glad to see her. They ran to her and hugged her as came up to the front door.

"Memere, Memere, how wonderful to see you," Cecile said. She was like a puppy who had been let out of a locked room.

"How wonderful to see you, too, my darling. How are you and Betty?"

"We're fine. We pick apples and feed the cows and chickens."

"I feed the chickens by myself," Betty said.

"That's wonderful," she said, relieved to see the girls were all right.

She turned to the farmer who was sitting in a chair near the fire.

"Are they well behaved?"

"Oh yes, they are no trouble. They are quiet and sad, but they are no trouble."

"They miss their father who is working to send for them, you know."

"Yes, that is what you said. I feel sorry for a man who had to leave his children to the care of others. I hope he sends for them soon."

"He will, just as soon as he finds work and can afford to bring them."

The adults talked for a few more minutes and then Memere spent the rest of the time with the girls. She was encouraged to see no signs of problems and happy to hear the girls tell her all was well.

The farmer's wife told Memere of the visit by the soldiers and asked if any such visit took place where she lived. Memere said there were no signs of any soldiers and that was fine with her. This was still French soil and the sight of German soldiers was a constant reminder of how their beautiful country was being occupied. She obviously didn't mention the other reason.

Memere stayed an hour, had coffee with the farmer's wife and then left. She kissed and hugged both children before she left and told them to be good and to remember what she had told them. She even put her finger to her lips so Cecile could see when the farmer's wife was turned around. She said she'd be back in a short time to check on the girls and tell of news from their father.

The girls went to bed early that night and by the time they awoke, it was already time for their morning chores. Cecile and Betty went out the front door and began to feed the chickens who were eagerly waiting for their breakfast.

Later that morning the farmer came in for an early lunch. Cecile and Betty were still in the yard, half feeding the other animals and half playing with them. Cecile decided to go inside to get a sweater Memere had brought for her. She was still in their room when the farmer sat down to eat.

He noticed his wife was not herself.

"Are you still nervous about the soldiers?" the farmer asked his wife.

"As a matter of fact, I am. I don't like that they were here and I'm not sure why they chose our house."

"Perhaps they were doing what they said, going to each house to talk about criminals and Jews."

"Why would they think we would know any Jews?"

"I just think they were talking to everyone. As a warning."

"I just wonder. You know the girls were very nervous when they came. Little Cecile could barely hold her spoon. She even dropped it once. She was very frightened."

"Well," the farmer said, "maybe they were frightened of the uniform. You know this is still new to the children. They all are seeing something they've never seen before."

"I wonder if that's just it. I wonder if there isn't something more. There's something odd about the Boisgointiers bringing them here. How sad they looked, like they had seen some kind of horror. They just don't seem right."

"Oh come now. There's nothing odd about two little girls being frightened of soldiers."

"I'm not so sure."

Cecile heard the farmer and his wife talking and tried to stay very still. She didn't want the farmer or his wife to know she was there. She leaned against wall and tried not to breathe.

"Well, next time you see Lucie ask her about the children."

"I don't know if I can wait until I see her next."

"But we took their money."

"Forget their money. If there's something wrong about those children, then all the money in the world won't mean anything."

"Well, what do you want to do?"

"I think I'm going to go to the police and tell them there is something strange about the children."

Cecile nearly fell to the floor. This was the worst thing she could hear. The farmer's wife was going to go to the police!

"I don't think you need to do that," the farmer said, finishing his lunch.

"I think I do. I haven't slept much since the soldiers came. I've been worried they are watching us and if the girls are children of criminals or worse we have to turn them in."

"What do you think two little girls could be?" he said. He thought the whole thing was a bit silly.

"They might be Jews. If they are then we have had them in our house, sleeping in our blankets, eating from our table and worse, we have been hiding them. Yes, I think I am going to go to the police. Maybe we can even get some money from the Germans."

"Well, if it will make you feel better, go to the police. They'll bring the soldiers here, the girls will tell them about their father and that will be it. I think it's all a little crazy."

"Well, I am going to go. I'll go tomorrow morning after breakfast."

Cecile couldn't move. She went back into the room and got the rest of her things and Betty's things. She opened the window and dropped the things on the floor. She climbed up and jumped out. It wasn't far. She ran to the side of the house and dropped hers and Betty's things. In a panic, she ran around to where Betty was playing with the chickens.

"Betty, come with me."

"Where are we going?"

"Never mind. Just come with me. Do you hear me?"

"Yes, I hear you." She put the stick she was using to chase the chickens down and walked with Cecile to the side of the house.

"We have to go. Don't say anything to me, we just have to go."

"Why do we have to go?"

"I think the farmer and his wife are bad people. They are going to tell those soldiers about us."

Betty took a quick breath in. Her eyes lit up with fear.

"Oh no Cecile. Remember what Memere said."

"I know. That's why we have to leave. Here you hold your bag and let's go into the fields."

Cecile began to lead Betty into the field around the side of the house. Suddenly she stopped cold in her tracks and put her hand to her mouth.

"My bag." She had left her bag in her room; She could not go anywhere without her pictures and her doll. How could she leave that behind? What was worse, she thought that if she left it behind they would find it and know they were Jews.

"I have to go back. Betty, you go to the back end of the field and wait for me. Go to the wall and sit there. I will be back in one minute."

"No Cecile, don't go back, they will catch you."

"Just go. I will be right back. Go now!" With fear in her eyes, Betty headed out towards the far end of the property.

Cecile decided to go back into the house through the front door. She hoped the farmer wouldn't know she left through the window. She took a few deep breaths and opened the door.

The farmer's wife was still cleaning up from her husband's lunch.

"What are you doing Cecile?"

"Oh nothing. Betty and I are picking apples from the trees at the end of the field."

"I don't think we need any more apples today, Cecile."

"Well, we'll only pick a few. We like it over by the trees. We chase the birds."

"Alright, but come back when it starts to get dark."

"We will," Cecile said and went into her room. She picked up her bag and put it in her pocket. She put her little doll inside her pocket, too and waited to hear the farmer's wife go to another side of the room. When she did, Cecile ran out the front door and back out into the front yard. She thought the farmer's wife might be watching so she decided to skip into the field like there was nothing wrong. All the while though, her heart raced and beat heavily. Her eyes were wide open and she hummed out of near panic. At least she made it out of the farmer's house.

The farmer's wife watched her skip into the field. "There's something wrong with those children. Why were they left up here. Why couldn't they stay somewhere else, like Paris. I wonder if they are Jews. I wonder if that Lucie Boisgointier knew they were Jews and tried to hide them here." She though she might not even wait until tomorrow to go to the police. She might go today. She thought about it again and decided there was too much to do today. Tomorrow morning, though, she would definitely tell the police she thought someone had hidden Jews with them without their knowledge.

Cecile found Betty huddled against the far wall in the field. Her eyes lit up when Cecile came out of the brush. She held Betty very tight.

"We have to get away right now. They know we are Jewish and they are going to tell the police."

"Where are we going to go?"

"We've got to find Memere. We've got to tell her so they can run away with us. Come on"

Cecile stood up and lifted Betty over the wall. She climbed over it herself and started to run.

"Wait," Cecile said to Betty who was several feet in front of her.

"Give me your hand." Betty lifted her small hand and Cecile gripped it tightly. "Let's go."

The two girls ran into an adjacent field and headed out. They didn't know where Memere lived and Cecile would only recognize some of the places around them. They stayed in the fields but followed the road as best they could. They would find Memere and she would protect them.

"Are they chasing us Cecile?" Betty asked each time Cecile looked behind.

"Not yet, Betty. But they will."

Cecile and Betty would learn many times to look over their shoulders. They were alone. They were scared. Now they were running away. How life could change, even for little girls.

Chapter Eight

Cecile and Betty ran as fast as they could. They weren't sure where they were running to, they just wanted to get as far from the farmer and his wife as possible. Cecile made sure they didn't cross too many roads or go near any house. They cut through fields and when they stopped to rest, they made sure it was along the rocks which separated one field from the other. While Cecile was older than Betty, she made sure to run at the younger girl's pace and to rest only when Betty couldn't run any more.

"When do we get to Memere?" Betty asked frequently. "I'm tired."

"I'm tired too, Betty. But we can't let anyone see us until we get to Memere's."

Cecile tried to remember any landmarks they passed that first day on their way to the farmer's house. There was a little stone bridge at the crossing of two roads that she recognized. They passed the landmark and quickly ran over the road and into the field next to the bridge. Cecile couldn't shake the feeling that the farmer's wife would soon know they weren't picking apples in their field and would rush to tell the police the little girls had ran away.

The dread of being caught kept Cecile moving. She didn't

want to tell Betty what trouble they would be in if they were found, but the haunting sight of the people being taken from the train by the soldiers wouldn't leave her. The anger of the soldiers that came to their apartment in Paris was as clear as if it happened yesterday. But the worst was having the two German soldiers come to the farmhouse. They were so close to them. Cecile could see their faces very clear. She thought of the one with the bad teeth who didn't say much and the other, the man in charge, who told the farmer's wife about the criminals and Jews. If they found her and her sister, what would they do to them? Cecile didn't want to get caught before her Mama or Papa would come to rescue them. Getting to Memere's without being seen was all that mattered to Cecile now. That and, of course, making sure she and Betty were together. That would push them, even when they were too tired to take another step.

"I'm hungry," Betty said. "When can we eat?"

"There's nothing to eat here, Betty, but maybe we can find some apples and eat them. They were so delicious, weren't they?"

"Yes. They were very good. I wish we had them now."

"I know," Cecile said. "Let's think about what we'll have to eat when we get back to Memere's."

"I want some biscuits—and potatoes," said Betty.

"Biscuits and potatoes? What kind of dinner will that be?"

"My dinner," Betty said with a gleeful little laugh.

"Maybe Memere will have some chicken for us, or even rabbit. With some cabbage, too. I would love that," Cecile said, looking around and readying herself for the next part of their journey.

Looking over the field, Cecile decided to take a path past the little church in the distance. She thought it looked familiar and there was some thick brush nearby. They would cross the road and get into the field behind it.

They crouched by the road and waited until they were sure there was no one around. As they ran across the road a car came around the curve to their left and headed their way. Cecile heard the car just before it came into view and took Betty's hand and ran to the other side of the road. As soon as they got there, Cecile pulled Betty down and they laid on the ground until the car passed. Without stopping, the car sped by. It didn't stop, but Cecile couldn't help wondering if the driver saw them and was just now driving to the police.

"Come on, let's go, Betty," Cecile said taking her sister by the hand. "We have to hurry up."

A while later they saw railroad tracks. They might have been the same tracks their train rode on. Cecile thought that by following near the tracks they would get to the station. At least then they would know where they were and would only have to follow the road towards the beach and Memere's house.

The tracks were in the middle of nowhere. There was no one around and they were able to walk on them. The trip became easier. They were out of the rough and tumble landscape of the rocks and fields and they were able to go a little faster.

"What happens if a train comes?" Betty asked.

"Then we'll run to the side and lay down so no one see us."

"What if someone is looking out the window like we were?"

"Oh, don't worry, Betty. We'll hide in the field and lay with our heads down. No one will see us."

Cecile decided they would feel better if they sang a little. She chose a song to sing and started mouthing the words in almost a whisper. They walked on the tracks in the middle of an empty landscape, singing songs they knew and loved, barely able to hear each other. The sun was getting low in the sky and Cecile hoped they would find Memere before nighttime.

As they neared the station, there was noticeably more activity. There were more houses to be seen, more vehicles and more signs of life. They stopped and watched as two cars passed each other on the road two hundred yards away from them. In the distance they could see smoke rising into the air. It looked like fireplace smoke to Cecile and she thought the station was right around the bend. They walked carefully, trying to listen for any sound.

Gradually, Cecile heard a vibrating sound from the tracks. It was faint at first but soon got stronger and stronger. In a short time, she could even feel it. From up ahead, she saw wisps of smoke up in the air.

"Betty. The train is coming. Come with me."

She took her sister by the hand and ran into the thick under-brush in the nearby field. They hid and waited. Minutes later they could hear the sound of the train approaching. Cecile looked up and watched it approach. It looked like a giant mechanical worm coming straight at them.

"Don't move. Keep your head down, Betty," she instructed her sister. Betty dutifully obeyed.

Cecile couldn't help looking up as the train passed. It wasn't moving very fast at all. First the locomotive went by. It was excit-ing to watch. She looked carefully as each car passed. Cecile was actually able to look in and see people in their seats. Some were looking out the window. Some were looking straight ahead. There were men, women and even some children in the train. A few of them had newspapers in their hands. Cecile was jealous of them. They were all going someplace. Maybe they were going home. Maybe the children she saw were with their parents. None of them were lying on the ground in the brush, unsure of where to go, afraid of being seen, like she and her sister.

There were trains just like this one, all over Europe, taking people to places they wanted to go to. But there were other trains too—trains that picked up thousands of frightened Jews, jamming them into cattle cars with no water or food and very little air. Those trains were not taking families home, or fathers back to their daughters and sons. Those trains would make their last stops at places with names like Auschwitz, Sobibor, Bergen Belsen or Buchenwald. The passengers were not arriving home, although they were at the end of their journey. There would be no comforting smells of a kitchen at dinnertime and no warmth from an inviting fireplace, although there would be fires and there would be odors.

When the train was safely passed, the girls got up and cut across the field. They found the road leading from the station to the ocean. Cecile recognized the road and for the first time was confident they would find Memere's house. It was a good thing, too. The sun was starting to go down and if they didn't hurry, darkness would overtake them.

They started to run again, trying to get to Memere's as fast as they could. Once or twice they had to take the road and they were afraid they would be seen, so close to Memere's. As soon as possible, they darted back into the field, laying still every time they thought there was someone approaching.

Cecile's heart started to race when they saw the path leading to Memere and Pepere. She even saw the little stone house in the distance.

"Please be there," Cecile thought to herself. "Please be home." She was very much afraid the farmer's wife had already told the police. They would certainly come looking for Memere and Pepere. She prayed they hadn't gotten there already.

They ran down the path towards the house. Cecile even ran ahead of Betty.

"Memere! Pepere!" Cecile and Betty both cried as they got near the house. They knocked on the door as hard as they could.

The door quickly opened and Memere stood in the doorway.

Both girls started to cry. Cecile first and then her sister.

"We found you. We found you," Cecile bellowed. "We were so lost and didn't know how to find our way back here."

"Cecile, what's happened?" Memere asked. Her voice expressed both relief and fear. She bent down and hugged both girls. They were both filthy and exhausted. They couldn't get the words out fast enough to tell Memere why they were there.

The other children were at the door as well and within seconds, Pepere appeared.

"Girls, why are you here? What happened at the farmhouse?"

"Oh Pepere, they know we are Jews and they are going to tell the police and the soldiers who came to the house that they had us. They wanted to get money for telling the soldiers," Cecile blurted out.

"So you ran away. Do they know you are gone. Did they see you?" Memere asked.

"No, Memere. They think we went to the field to pick apples. We ran as fast as we could. She said she was going to go to the police in the morning."

"Oh my God," Memere said, holding her hand to her mouth. "It's getting dark now, they must have already realized you are not in the field. They might have already tried to go to the police. Georges, now what do we do?"

"Did we do wrong, Memere?" Cecile wanted to know.

Memere looked at the two little girls. They had been through more than their share of heartaches. They had seen so much and had so little left.

"No my darling. You did the right thing. Your parents would be very proud of you."

"Grandmother and grandfather, too?" Betty said.

"Yes, your grandparents would be proud of you as well."

Memere stood up and brought the children inside. She took Cecile and Betty and washed them and cleaned their clothing as best she could. All the while Cecile told the story of the soldiers, the farmer's conversation with his wife and their escape. Memere sat was amazed at their journey through unfamiliar places and the young girls' ability to find her and Georges again, especially from such a distance. She had the girls sit down and eat with the others. Once the food was on the table, Memere and Pepere went into the other room. They could hear the children tell the others about their predicament and their heroic escape.

"Now what?" Georges said to his wife.

"They will most certainly tell the police where the girls came from. They could be driving up this road any time."

"Yes, you're right about that. We could be jailed tonight. Or worse," Georges said.

Memere walked around the room very nervously. She was thinking very fast.

"We cannot stay here, Georges," she finally decided. "We will be discovered. There is no doubt. It will mean our lives and these children's' lives. We've got to leave. Tonight. Right now."

Georges nodded his head in agreement. There was a short moment of silence as they looked at each other. Each one was trying to decide what to do to get away as fast as possible.

"I'll get the children ready. Why don't you gather what we need and we'll leave right after they've eaten," Memere said, taking control of the situation.

"Where should we go?" Georges questioned.

"I'm not sure. I think I know a place. We can go to Mehoudin and see Father Louis. He will hide us and help us get a place to live."

"Are you sure about that? We are coming to him with quite a group."

"I'm sure. He won't turn us away."

Memere quickly went into the other room where the children were having dinner. Cecile was still telling her story and everyone seemed excited and frightened by the tale. Betty was sitting next to her, adding to the escape story wherever she could.

"Children, we must pack up our things right now," Memere told them. She tried to be comforting as she told them but her words put fear in most of the youngsters.

"Where are we going?" one asked.

"I'm frightened," said another.

"Don't worry my darlings. It will be all right. We just have to pack and leave now. The farmer and his wife know where we live and they will surely bring the Gestapo here. Our lives are at risk and we must leave here tonight and get to somewhere safe."

Outside, Pepere was readying as much as he could for the trip. Without a car, they would all have to walk to safety. As it was dark, they could not trust the roads because they would be out in the open in the event the police were coming to their house. They would have to walk.

Pepere shook his head as he emptied the wheelbarrow. He would put as many belongings in it as he could. Most of the children would have to walk and the older ones would take turns helping to push the wheelbarrow. He hoped the farmers in the nearby houses would not see them, for the police and Gestapo would have an easy time getting them to tell which way they went.

He brought out as many things as the wheelbarrow would hold. None of the children, snatched in the nick of time, had many possessions, so their things would be easy. He and Lucie would have to leave most of what they owned and just take what they would absolutely need.

Meanwhile, Memere was getting all the children dressed and ready to leave. Each one seemed to need special attention to quiet their fears and to make them feel secure about their pending journey. Cecile and Betty already had everything they owned with them so they helped the others pack up.

Memere took as much food off the shelves as she could. While she felt sure they would be taken in by the priest, she was making sure and whatever could be readied to travel was taken.

Georges came in and told her they were ready to go.

"It's time for us to leave, everyone. Are you all ready to go?" There was a chorus of "Yes, Pepere."

"What about the animals, Georges?" Memere said.

"Well we certainly cannot bring them with us," he responded.

"What do you mean we cannot bring them? They have to come with us. They can't stay here."

"Lucie, we can't take the chance the dog will bark or that the cats will meow or that any of them will run away from us if we are in any danger. We have to leave them here. It will make it seem more likely we are coming right back."

"I am not leaving these animals here for the Nazis to find them. They are coming with us."

Pepere looked at her for a long time. The room was silent as each child waited for the discussion's conclusion. The dog and the cats were more than pets, they were a symbol for each of them. Their softness and innocence were important for these children who had seen everything else in their lives taken away from them.

"Georges, we can't go without them," Memere said quietly.

"All right," he said with resignation. "We'll bring them with us."

In spite of all the danger that faced them, every one of the eight children broke into big smiles as they felt the relief of not having to leave the animals behind. Memere just stood there and slowly shook her head up and down. Cecile helped load the cats into a box while another child fashioned a homemade leash for the dog.

Both Memere and Pepere took last looks around the tiny house to make sure they had everything they needed.

"Let's go everyone. Come on, out back," Pepere said.

Once outside, they added to the mound growing in the wheelbarrow. It was quite high and Pepere wasn't sure it would even move, let alone be pushed mile after mile through fields and over rocks.

"Children," Memere said. "Come here." The youngsters all gathered around her.

"It is going to be very dangerous where we are going. Once we get there it will be fine. But we have a long way to go and Pepere will need help in pushing the wheelbarrow. Each of you must be absolutely quiet all the way there. When you see me put my finger to my mouth, you must be extra quiet. Silent. No one must know we are walking through the fields or they will tell the Nazis we are here. It's very important that we are not found. It's important to all of us and it's important to each of your parents. They wanted all of you to be safe from the Nazis and the only way that will happen is if you are each quiet as mice. So there will be no more talking until we get there and I want each of you to hold hands with someone else."

Cecile took Betty's hand very tightly as she listened to Memere. Betty returned the grip. Memere wondered how they would get all the way to Mehoudin. But she knew the Gestapo would arrive shortly and there was no choice. Fortunately, there was enough of a moon in the sky and their way would at least be somewhat lit. Lucky for the moon, she thought. She was amazed at the children, how wide their little eyes stared back at her as she gave them the important final instructions. She bent down and kissed each child, telling every one not to worry and that they would be all right. Memere, Pepere and the menagerie would need a great deal of luck and help this night if they were to make it to the morning.

"All right, everyone," Pepere finally whispered. "It's time to go." He struggled to get the wheelbarrow moving. They would have to be on the road for a while otherwise they would leave a trail right from their house. Memere walked silently, looking ahead at Cecile and Betty. She hoped the Gestapo wouldn't care all that much about two little girls.

Chapter Nine

Looking like a traveling circus, Memere and her family made their way through the fields, heading towards Mehoudin where they hoped to find safety. Over and over again, the wheelbarrow with all their belongings tipped and food, clothing and supplies fell out. Patiently and silently, Memere picked everything up and helped get it started again.

Pepere pushed until he couldn't push any more and when he was too exhausted to go on, everyone rested. He regained his strength and started out again. If they could get to Father Louis' house before daybreak they would have the benefit of not being caught out in the open.

For their part, the children made the trek without causing any delays. Each carried as much as they could and the sound of shifting packages and footsteps was all that was heard. They dutifully waited to be told to rest and were prepared when Memere and Pepere told them to move on. Otherwise, they just pushed on. Memere knew the countryside and knew how to get to the priest's house through the desolate fields. But with a wheelbarrow and eight children and a group of animals, the going was slow and deliberate.

Memere and Pepere constantly tried to keep the pace quicker. Daylight would be their enemy and they would be easily exposed in the sunshine, even if they were out in the fields. So they continued to push on.

Cecile walked near the rear of the group, holding Betty's hand. In their other hands, they each held their own little satchel. Cecile kept reaching into her jacket to touch her little doll and the pocket book of pictures and memories she took from Paris. Betty still had the homemade doll her sister made for her in the hospital as they waited for their mother.

Much of those days seemed distant to Cecile and Betty. It was months since the Nazis burst into their apartment and changed their lives forever. There had been so much activity, so many changes of locations, new people, close calls and fear that they had become different people. Both girls clung to the hope that their parents would be coming for them, but they had since learned that they would have to participate in their own survival. Walking silently through these fields at 3am was only one of many examples.

Cecile often wondered what had happened to her father and sister after she and Betty went with their mother. But she had no clue. She had no ideas. Perhaps they were taken to jail. Maybe they were released and were home right now. There was no way for an 11 year old to even imagine the horrors that people were subjected to in these times. Instead, she clung to hope.

Pepere needed to rest and he stopped. He whispered to the children to sit down for a while.

"How far are we, Lucie?" Pepere asked his wife.

"I think we have about a mile to go."

"I hope so. I don't know how much longer I can push this." Pepere looked up at the sky and saw the first faint signs of daybreak coming on.

Memere gave each child a biscuit and some water from the wheelbarrow. Each one ate hungrily. She even gave one to the dog. It was important for her to keep the children's spirits high and the smile on her face seemed to do that.

"When we get to the house, you'll wait in the field with the children and I'll go in and talk to Father Louis," Memere said to Pepere. "I'll tell him the story and then we'll come out for you."

"I hope he can help," Pepere said. "If he doesn't, we are in deep trouble."

"He will, Georges. He has to. He won't just leave us here to be picked up. After all, he's a priest and he's still French."

"Let's keep moving," Pepere said. The traveling menagerie prepared to move out.

They moved through the fields slowly and deliberately—through one and into another. They all seemed alike and as they edged closer to Father Louis' church, the terrain seemed to get more difficult to cross.

As they passed over the rocks separating one field from another, almost within eyesight of the church, the wheelbarrow tipped over and everything fell out. The group was exhausted and the prospect of having to repack was not a happy one for anybody. But with care, Pepere put everything back in, fitting all the items perfectly. Some of the children slept as they sat on the ground. Memere held little Rene who was crying. She was trying to console him, to make him stop sobbing. Within a few moments of being held in her loving arms, he stopped his little cries and drifted off to sleep.

Unfortunately for Rene, he was starting to relax just at the time when the wheelbarrow was fully loaded and again they had to move out. It was a good thing they were getting close, the morning was starting to reveal its gray sky. If the Gestapo had chosen to look for Georges and Lucie last night, their house would have already been ransacked. If they waited for morning, it was likely to happen right about then.

The group finally came to a field near a road. They walked through it more carefully than through any of the others, for in the distance they could see an occasional car rumbling down the road. Their lights were still on but Pepere was worried that soon the night would totally disappear and they would be out in the open. They tried to hurry to the end of the field where there were trees and hedges for them to hide in.

They got to the bushes just a few dozen yards from the road and Memere put her finger to her mouth. The children knew that they had to be absolutely silent now as they could be caught at any moment. Just on the other side of the road, down a path was Father Louis' house and Memere could see it.

"You wait here with the children," Memere whispered to her husband. "I'm going to the house and try to find Father Louis. We'll come back and bring everyone to the house."

"If you have any trouble, find a way to let me know. I'll be watching from here."

Memere crawled over to Cecile and came very close to her ear. "I'm going to see my friend and he will bring us into his house. You must not say a word and you must make sure none of the other children do either. Just put you finger to your mouth and they will listen to you."

"Alright Memere," Cecile whispered back. "We won't say a word."

Memere looked at Pepere and waited to be sure there were no cars coming. She walked out of the bushes and headed across the road and down the path to the priest's house.

The struggle through the fields had taken its toll on Memere's clothing and she looked like she had been walking through muddy fields in the dark. She tried to brush herself off so that even if a car came by, it would appear that she was a farmer's wife out for a walk in the morning light. No matter how she tried to clean herself off, she stayed filthy. She breathed heavily as she walked quickly down the path. "Please let him be in," she thought to herself. They had come so far and were in such great danger.

Memere knocked on the priest's door. Six am is very early for there to be a friendly knock on the door. But Father Louis was used to it. His parishioners would often come to his house when someone was very sick or a child was born or for a host of matters that called for divine involvement. Still, she had to knock several times.

After what seemed an eternity the door opened. Father Louis, still in his night clothes was quite surprised to see Memere standing in doorway.

"Lucie Boisgointier! What are you doing here? So far from home and so early."

"Father Louis, I am in great danger,"

The priest looked at her. He looked at her clothing. He saw the anguish in her face and brought her into the house very quickly.

"Lucie. Sit down please. I'll put some coffee on."

Memere walked to the couch in the priest's sitting room. She was exhausted and struggled to keep herself awake as he put the coffee up. As she fought back sleep, she thought of Pepere and the children hiding in the bushes across the road. She would have to tell the priest everything.

Father Louis came back in and sat down next to her.

"Lucie. Tell me what trouble you are in."

Memere took a deep breath and told him the entire story. She told him about the parents begging her to take their children to safety and her grabbing them just as the Nazi's were taking them away. She told him about going to the city alone and returning by train with youngsters too frightened to move and nearly in shock. She told him about Cecile and Betty and Rene and the rest. He listened attentively with no expression other than kindness and respect on his face. She began to break into tears when she told him of taking Cecile and Betty to the farmer's house and how they were about to turn the little girls in, hopefully for a reward.

"Father, we had to leave our house. We're sure the farmer went to the police and we are more than sure the Gestapo has been to our house or will be there any minute. If they found us they would have killed Georges and me and the children. We had to get away."

"Where are Georges and the children, Lucie?" the priest gen-

tly asked. He tried to make Memere feel she made the right decision coming to him and even more importantly, that she was safe
in his house.

"They are across the road, hiding in the field. We loaded
everything onto a wheelbarrow and Georges pushed it all the way
here. The children were so wonderful. They didn't say a word. We
walked all the way, sometimes carrying the littlest ones, sometimes all of us had to push the cart."

Father Louis could plainly see the anguish in her face. She
didn't ask anything of him but he already knew what he would do.

"Lucie. Let's go back outside and get them. We'll bring everyone in here. You'll all be safe here."

"Oh Father. I didn't know where else to go. I don't want you
to be involved in this but I have nowhere else to turn."

"Don't say anything, Lucie. We know what we have to do.
God would want us to be charitable in this way and sacrifice the
way you have. He'll watch over us and we'll be fine. The children
had nowhere to turn and they somehow were led to you. You had
nowhere to turn and were led here. We'll all turn to the Lord and
there is no safer place to turn."

Father Louis was amazed at Lucie's story. He knew her to be
a strong woman, a wonderful woman. But he hadn't thought of
her in this light before. She was heroic in his eyes. To take the
risks she took was truly remarkable and everyone who would now
play a role in her journey should be privileged to be given a part
to play.

"Come with me Lucie. Let's bring them in. Daylight has
arrived and they need to be indoors. We'll wait for the coffee until
we're all inside."

Memere and Father Louis walked out of the house. If anyone
had seen them it would just appear that priest and parishioner
were walking as they talked. Memere was very nervous about
walking back with all the children in tow.

They decided they would leave the wheelbarrow in the field

and bring the group to the house. Later, Father Louis would go back for the cart.

When they got to the spot where Georges and the children were they found each of them fast asleep. They were huddled together around Pepere and looked so innocent. As innocent as they looked, they were completely vulnerable.

Memere woke Pepere and then each child. She awoke them with a kiss and gently shook them out of their sleep.

"Children, come with us. This is Father Louis."

"Hello, Father. Thank you," Georges said.

"I am happy to see you, Georges," the priest said, "especially after what you've been through these past months."

"I'm fine, father. The children have been through much worse."

"Come children, let's get into the house. It's just over there," the charitable priest said.

The group stood up and waited as Father Louis looked up the road.

"Come. We can go. But we need to move quickly."

It wasn't very far to the priest's house, but there was nowhere to hide and nowhere to turn. What's more, there were few stories that could be concocted as to why the priest, eight children and pets were walking down the road at such an early hour. As they got to Father Louis' path, everyone started to run.

They nearly burst into the front door. Some of the children immediately went for the couches. They all found somewhere to lay down and within minutes, were asleep.

"Georges, Lucie, come with me into the kitchen," Father Louis said. "We have much to discuss. When they wake up we'll make them something to eat. In the meantime, let them rest."

Memere looked back at them as she left the room. They had made it to the priest and she believed he would not turn his back on them.

Father Louis, Memere and Pepere sat in the kitchen for

hours trying to determine what to do next. There were eight children, a dog and several cats to worry about, not to mention Memere and Pepere. They would need to be a part of the community but not be identifiable. The children would have to go to school, as Catholics of course, and there must be no sign of them being Jewish. The priest would see to it that they would all have papers indicating their religion and they would have to pass as Memere's children.

In the priest's little village, there was very little German presence and if all went well they would be forgotten about. They hoped that when the Gestapo got to Memere's house, they would assume they had gone to Paris or another larger city and they would have neither the time nor the will to look for them. Besides, the Nazi's didn't know how many children were with Memere and they would not look very hard for the two young girls who were with the Boisgointiers. They would just assume they fell through the cracks.

The first thing Father Louis needed to do was to feed the Boisgointiers. Then he would have to find them a place to live.

"Lucie, Georges. You must relax. I will help you and no one will ever know your secret from me. It's time for you to sleep as well. Please, stay here and don't go out of the house and don't answer the door."

The children all slept well into the afternoon while Memere and Pepere finally were able to sleep once their discussion with the priest ended. As they slept, the priest left. He left a note saying he was going to the village to tend to some details and would return soon. Had they been awake when he left, Memere and Pepere might have worried about whether the priest was actually keeping his word to them. Before leaving, he laid out food for them so once they awoke they would be able to eat.

One by one the youngsters awoke. They tried to be quiet so that Memere and Pepere could sleep too but it was to no avail. They were, after all, children, and in a short time, the adults were up too.

"Are you hungry children?" Memere asked as she sat up.

Almost in unison, the youngsters said they were. Memere got up and went to the kitchen where Father Louis had put out food.

"Come children, there is breakfast for you."

They didn't need to be asked a second time. They crowded around the small table and ate what had been left at the table. It was as if they had not eaten for days.

"Memere," Cecile said. "Are we safe here?" As the oldest, Cecile was also the one who most understood the situation. "Will the Nazis know to come looking for us?"

"I don't think they will look for us, but we mustn't give them any reason to suspect us. Father Louis will find us a place to live and we will become like everyone else. You'll go to school and we'll all be one big family. As far as everyone will know, you are all our children and we came here together from Orly."

"But what if they come for us, Memere?"

"Well, my darling. We can't think of that. We must only think of living here and being part of this nice little village."

After they ate, Memere gathered all the children together and sat them down. She told them that they were fine in the priest's house and that the priest was going to try and find them a house of their own. They would, she said, grow their own food and those who were old enough would go to school. She also told them what to say if anyone asks about their parents. They were to say Memere and Pepere were their parents. Most of the children understood.

Memere had them sing several songs she knew. She did not want them to sing their own songs as she didn't want anyone to question the words in the songs. In fact, she told them never to sing their songs in public.

Cecile told herself that she would listen to Memere and not sing any of the songs she knew. But she told herself equally as surely that she would never forget her songs, like the ones she would sing with Papa on Sunday morning or especially, her treasured "Jattendrais," the one song she most associated with him. She explained to Betty why they couldn't sing like they did at the hospital while they waited for Mama. Betty didn't understand why they couldn't sing but she would listen to Cecile and Memere.

Late in the day, as night was falling, they saw Father Louis walking down the path pushing the wheelbarrow that contained all their belongings. He brought it around back and came into the house. In his arms was a bundle of food and other items.

"Good evening everyone. I hope everybody had a chance to eat and you are feeling very good."

The children all nodded but none would speak. They didn't quite know if they could trust this man. None had much contact with priests in their short lives. Cecile thought that he was like a rabbi and decided she would think of the priest in the same way as the Rebbe in Paris.

He laid out more food for the evening and the children swarmed around it.

"I found you all a little house to live in near the railroad tracks. You will have to lift the gates for the train from time to time, but you'll be all right there."

He explained to Memere and Pepere that they would live in the little house and would be gatekeepers for the trains. They would have the schedule and would know when the gates would have to come up and then put back down.

He also had papers for each of the children, identifying them as Boisgointiers and as Catholics. In fact, Cecile even received her Holy Communion. As respectful as she was of Memere's faith, she never lost sight of the fact that she was Jewish and understood clearly she was being shielded by this warm and caring Catholic priest.

They would need to carry their papers in the event anyone inquired about them. But they would be fine and could learn to relax a little. Father Louis said he would take them to their new home in the morning.

Memere and Pepere examined the papers carefully and Memere put them in her bag.

"I think we'll be safe, Georges," Memere said to her husband.

"I hope you are right," he said. He was amazed at how much their life had changed and they weren't even Jewish.

Before going to sleep Cecile came over to Memere.

"Don't worry about us, Memere. We'll be good."

"I know you will my darling."

"I'll take care of Betty. She will always be with me. We'll help with the others."

"Thank you. We still need to be very careful."

"What if my parents come for us? How will they know where to find us?"

"Cecile, we have to wait for the Germans to leave. I don't think your parents will try to come for you as long as the Nazis are here. We'll just wait for them to leave and we'll worry about your parents then. They know you are safe and they know you are being good for them. In the meantime, you'll go to school and learn and make them very proud. When you are all together again, you can tell them all about your adventures. How does that sound?"

"That sounds okay. I'll have lots to tell them. So will Betty. Good night, Memere. I love you."

"I love you too, Cecile," Memere said. She gave the young girl a tight hug. She could barely hold back her own tears. What would happen to her and Betty? What would happen to any of them? They all held out hope they would see their parents again. Memere knew it would take a miracle. In these days, with Nazis all around, a war blazing in Europe, Africa, the Pacific, in Russia and in so many other places, miracles were hard to come by. She would take care of these children. She swore to God she would and nothing was going to stop her from doing that.

"Come my darling, go lay down near Betty. You need to sleep.

Tomorrow will be a busy day." She picked up Cecile and carried her to bed. She knelt down and kissed each child on the forehead and said "I love you" to each. If nothing else, she wanted each little one to feel cared for. Maybe that would make them a little less frightened.

By the time she got into the kitchen with Pepere and Father Louis, she was completely overcome with sadness.

Chapter Ten

Memere, Pepere and all the children walked with Father Louis to the house by the railroad tracks. It was a ramshackle, two room box off the road with no lights, no running water and no bathrooms. The tracks passed very close to the house and there was a big gate that had to be closed whenever a train went by. There was a well nearby which would provide the water they needed and an outhouse for going to the bathroom. The conditions were, by any definition, primitive.

Pepere brought the things from the wheelbarrow into the house and Memere tried to clean things up and make it look a little like home.

"I have to go back to the church now," Father Louis said. "You'll be safe here. I will register the children for school next week and you must get them used to saying they are not Jews. Tell them to stay away from anyone in a uniform and just stay away from anything that looks like trouble."

"Thanks, Father," Pepere said. He held out his hand. "Thank you for everything."

"Georges, I am a priest and I am French. I could do nothing less than this and probably much more. In the meantime, we'll look to God for the ultimate deliverance."

"Will you come to see us?" Memere asked.

"Yes, I'll come every few days and I'll see the older ones at the school from time to time. Don't worry. We will all be fine."

Father Louis left the small house and headed back to the church. After he was gone, all 10 Boisgointiers just stood in silence as they looked around. There were no beds, just a couple of chairs. In the back there were a few pigs and a cow was in the field nearby.

It was a dismal place to live. But there was no choice. Everyone tried to settle in as best they could. Memere spent the entire day cleaning the house, with the help of Cecile. The little ones were assigned temporary jobs which made them feel busy. Pepere spent the day cutting firewood and bringing it into the house. By nightfall, the house was warm, there was food from the priest and a tired but thankful group settled down to dinner and sleep.

In the days and weeks that followed, life settled in for the Boisgointier clan. Cecile's main job was to tend to the gate when the train came by but she was also responsible for cleaning the clothes in the stream and to help cook the vegetables and rabbits. They made oil for their lamps from pigs' fat and it took quite some time for everyone to get used to the smell of it.

As difficult as it was by standards of the time, they found a way to accept it. They constantly told each other that they were lucky not to have been caught by the Nazis. This was heaven compared to what the Nazis would have done to them.

Each day Memere would take all the children to the church. Memere relied on the church as a place of solace, a sanctuary. She also wanted the people in the village to get used to seeing her in church and make the natural assumption they were all Catholics. She wanted the family to become part of the fabric of the community.

At night, Memere read to the children from the bible. A religious person, Memere wanted to give the children something spiritual, but more than that, wanted them to be familiar with a religion outside Judaism. The older children caught on quickly. The younger ones simply enjoyed the biblical stories.

Cecile started school. It was a single classroom school with children of varying ages attending. She was nervous on her first day. After all, she would be away from her protector, Memere, even if only for a few hours each day. She was living a life in hiding and had an identity that wasn't really her own.

Before her first day Memere took Cecile off to the side and spoke with her about going to school.

"I want you to enjoy going to school, Cecile. You must go and learn. But there are a few things I want to discuss with you."

"What are they Memere?"

"The first thing is that I want you to leave your little pocket book at home. You mustn't have that with you. I also think you should throw your Jewish star away. It would be too much of a chance to take."

Cecile was not happy at the idea of losing her star.

"Memere, do I have to throw away my Jewish star? I've had it since the Germans came into Paris. I have one, Betty has one, Marguerite has one and so do my mother and father. We all have them and I don't want to throw mine away."

"My darling if you are caught with the Jewish star we will all be in great trouble. We've been through so much already. Be a big girl and make sure we aren't caught."

Tears started to come to the little girl's eyes. Slowly, she shook her head. It was as if losing the star would mean removing her past. She just stood there, not wanting to defy Memere but not willing to give up the little yellow patch.

Memere looked at her and knew she couldn't ask her to do it. She dropped her eyes and gave in. She decided that there was only so much you can take from a person and you may simply not know what that person uses to shield their soul. In the case of this brave little twelve year old, the only connection with her lost family was in her heart, in her mind and in the heart of her young sister. The star was too important to her past for Memere to take away.

"Okay my darling. We don't have to throw it away. But we must be careful with it. I don't want you to carry it with you. I want you to hide it and don't tell Pepere where it is. Let's keep it between us for a while."

"Oh thank you, Memere," Cecile threw her arms around the woman. "I love you."

"I love you too, Cecile. Come. Let's find a hiding spot and then let's go to school."

Memere knew that she had to send Cecile to school and once out of her sight, might be vulnerable to being discovered. Her fears were for nothing. Cecile enjoyed school and was able to get along quite well. In fact, it seemed to energize her.

Cecile was welcomed warmly at the school. The teacher, Miss Simone, was an older woman, in her mid 50's. She had to be able to relate to children as young as eight all the way through high school age. It was a special skill to run a school with students with such a wide range of ages and life experiences.

The brick school building didn't look all that happy from the outside, but once in the door it was different. It was well decorated with drawings from the students and the signs of learning were everywhere—many books, maps, math problems and so on.

On her first day, Miss Simone introduced Cecile to the rest of the school.

"Students," she said as she brought a ragged looking young girl to the front of the class. Cecile was nervous as she felt the eyes of all 20 classmates on her. But there were no mean faces and no apparent anger in their eyes. "I want everyone to say hello to Cecile Boisgointier."

"Hello Cecile," the class repeated.

"Cecile just moved here with her family from Orly. We're happy to have you here Cecile."

Cecile wanted to say 'thank you' to the class but was too

embarrassed. She just smiled at everyone and gave a faint wave. One young girl, about her age, called to Cecile to sit by her. Cecile was glad to do it and thought she already had a friend. It wasn't like the last school she attended in which the children were so consumed with the hate taught by their parents that Cecile had to run away and not return.

She would come home from school and quickly tend to her chores. She would close the gate for the train as soon as she came home and then help the others pick the vegetables for supper. After supper, there was homework to do and reading by lamp-light. Sometimes Cecile would discuss her schoolwork with Memere. Betty was proud of her sister in school and talked about it often. She frequently said she couldn't wait until she was old enough to go to the small school.

Cecile learned much during this period. Pepere taught her how to catch a rabbit and skin it for dinner. Cecile hated this job. She felt very sad for the poor little animal. But to skin it and dry it and sell it in the village was the only way for the family to make any money and in time, she was able to do it without thinking. She would just think about something else until it was over.

As the weeks and months went by, life settled in for the Boisgointiers and the children. By many standards, life stayed difficult. Nights were hard as there were no beds for any of them. Everyone slept on the floor or on chairs. They covered themselves with potato sacks or spare clothing.

The time was taking its toll, though, on Pepere. He was becoming more sad and more distant with each passing month. His spirit was starting to break and cracks in his brave personality were beginning to show. It came to a head one day when Memere had gone to the village.

Cecile was making soup in the chimney when she realized she had forgotten to tend to the gates. She heard the whistle of the train and froze, realizing her mistake. She dropped the large wooden spoon on the table and ran out to the gate. Luckily, she was in time. She quickly opened it waited until the train arrived and for it to go by.

Happy in being able to get there in time, she skipped back into the house. Unfortunately, by the time she got back the soup had burned and had boiled over the side of the pot.

"Oh no," she cried, bringing her hands to her mouth. "Pepere is going to be so mad at me." She doused the fire in the chimney and in a panic ran out of the house. If only Memere hadn't gone to the village.

Cecile ran as fast as she could into the field and hid behind the rocks. Maybe Memere will come home and fix it. Maybe Pepere wouldn't notice. What would she do?

She had plenty of time to think about it as she stayed in the field for several hours. Finally, though, she had to return. She couldn't let Pepere think something had happened to her. That would frighten him too much and make it much worse. She decided to return.

She slowly walked back to the house and was overjoyed when she saw Memere in the firelight. She went into the house to tell Memere what happened. She didn't get very far.

"Cecile, come here. Where have you been and what in God's name happened to the soup," Pepere bellowed as she walked in.

Cecile tried to answer.

"Pepere, I'm...."

"You frightened me. I thought they had taken you," Pepere bellowed. "You know what your job is and you forgot to do it and scared us half to death."

"I forgot to open the gate and I....."

Before she could finish Pepere came towards her with his hands raised. Seeing this Memere tried to get between her husband and the child and Betty rushed to her sister. Pepere pushed Memere away and when she came back he hit her across the chest. Memere tumbled backwards over the chair.

"I ought to tear you limb from limb you ungrateful child.

Look at how we live, look at what we've become. I ought to beat you and beat you."

He took off his belt and began to whip Cecile. He hit her hard over and over again. Each time Memere got up to help, Pepere pushed her away and kept hitting Cecile. The other children had never seen Pepere like this and ran out of the house crying. He continued to hit the child until he became exhausted and fell back against the wall, slowly slumping to the ground.

Cecile laid on the floor in a heap. She was bleeding from several cuts and was sobbing. Betty threw herself on top of her sister. Memere picked her up and held her, glaring at her husband who seemed to be in shock himself.

"Oh my darling are you all right. Please don't cry. It's over now. Please my darling. I'm so sorry," Memere was nearly hysterical herself.

She brought Cecile to her bed and gently laid her on it. The little girl could not stop sobbing from the pain and the shock of what had just happened to her. Memere brought some cold water and began to gently cool the welts that had already started to show and to stop the bleeding.

Betty stood with her eyes wide open. She couldn't speak and couldn't move. Watching the blood all over her sister and seeing her in the midst of a beating had sent her into a feeling of terror, which took a long time to subside. In time she came over to the bed and began to help Memere tend to Cecile's wounds.

"Try not to cry, Cecile. I know it hurts but you must try to relax. Pepere didn't mean to hurt you but you frightened us so. Pepere loves you and would never hurt you on purpose."

"I'm sorry Memere. I'm sorry I forgot to close the gate and burned the soup."

"No, my darling. It was your running away that caused this. We are worried for our lives every day—and yours too. We thought you had been taken by the Nazis, or worse. We were scared for you and for all the other children, like Betty and Rene.

If they kidnapped you they could come and take the rest, and us too. But it's over now. They'll be no more hitting, ever."

Cecile just laid on the bed as Memere spent many hours cooling her wounds. It took her several days to heal. In a way though, that horrible event seemed to snap the tension that had been rising in Pepere. As Cecile healed, Pepere began to come back to his old self again. But try as she might, the youngster could not help keeping her distance from him. Her love for Memere and their relationship continued to grow, but she would always be wary of Pepere.

As life continued uneventfully, it was easy to lose sight of why they were there and what was at stake. There was an undercurrent of German presence but it didn't really interrupt their lives. They were tucked away in a small village up near the coast and the Germans were a lot more interested in what was going on in the big cities. The Boisgointier clan had no way of knowing what was going on around the world other than the local rumor mill. Since they didn't spend a great deal of time with others, they were more isolated than most. But as 1943 became 1944, everyone was used to their routine and the Germans were something people feared only when they thought about it. Life was too hard on its own.

But 1944 did not begin without its problems for Cecile. An accident in which the large pot filled with boiling water for washing fell on Cecile put her in a hospital for a few days. The burns had become infected and it looked for a while that she would have to lose her foot. Memere brought Cecile to a wealthier church parishioner who, along with Memere and Father Louis, helped nurse the young girl back to health. During her recuperation, Cecile spent time away from Betty for the first time in her life. The pain of separation was worse than the pain in her feet. It was hard for Betty, too. When her young sister visited her, Cecile had to explain that they were separated in order for her to get better. She also told Betty that she could visit her often, every day if she wanted and Memere did bring Betty every day. The fact that the parishioner gave Cecile her own room, her own bed, warm blankets and all she could eat made her more comfortable but didn't make her feel better. She couldn't bear to be separated from Betty and welcomed the time when she could go back.

She returned with her injuries tended and with a great deal of food that she talked the parishioner into letting her take home. It was a time for celebration as the Boisgointiers were treated to their best meal in all the time they were in hiding.

Soon though, the memory of an enormous meal faded and the family returned to their day to day life. Cecile continued to go to school and they went to church every day. They lived quietly, but had made friends of the villagers and truly felt they belonged.

A booming knock interrupted the family shortly after dinner. Cecile and Betty froze, as did Memere and Pepere. It wasn't the first time there was a knock on their door, but this knock had the sound of danger.

"Who is there," Memere said tentatively.

"It's me," Father Louis said. Memere and Pepere looked at each other. This was not Father's usual knock. Pepere opened the door.

"Come in Father," Pepere said, but the priest flew by him before he could get the words out.

"We must pack up the children right now and they must come back with me."

"What's the matter?" Memere asked.

"It's the Nazis. They are here."

"Oh My God," Memere moaned as she crossed herself. "Where are they?"

"They are in Normandy and are sweeping the countryside looking for Jews."

"Do they know about us?"

"I don't know if they know about you but they are looking for hidden Jews and are taking those they find away into the fields.

Some have said the Germans are shooting them."

"Oh, no. What do we do?" Memere stood up and grabbed Cecile.

"I will take the children with me. You stay here. You must hide any sign that there are more than the two of you here and when they come, you mustn't say anything about them. This is not a local sweep so they will not know who was here and who wasn't. You must make it look like you are a couple whose job it is to tend the gate. I'll take the children with me."

"Come children, we must move quickly." Memere began to get the children ready while Pepere and Father Louis began to hide the young ones' belongings, hiding any sign of them. Some of the children started to cry from the sheer panic in the room. Cecile panicked not only from the intense activity but she knew what was likely to be coming.

"Memere, I'll make sure the children are all right. We know how to be quiet and we will not say a word."

"That's good Cecile," she said as she dressed the little ones.

"How far away are they?" Pepere asked.

"They are sweeping through Normandy now which means we probably have an hour or two. We have to move quickly. It will still take us some time to get to the church."

In minutes the children were ready. Memere decided to go with Father Louis to take the children to the church. There would be no time for stopping and the littlest ones would likely need to be carried. Memere was sure to take all the papers the priest had forged for the children. They may at least offer some protection if they were found.

"Georges, make sure all signs of them are hidden. Keep looking around and around. Make sure you look outside too."

"Don't worry about that. Just make sure you get to the church safely."

"Come," Father Louis said. "We've got to leave now."

Memere grabbed her own coat and they walked out the door.

Each child tried not to cry, but they were very scared. Each who could remember was reminded of another rousing out of their homes. Memere looked at Cecile and with her eyes asked if her little satchel was well hidden. Cecile nodded that it was hidden away.

They practically ran down the road and once again darted into the fields. They would have to take several chances in order to get to the church quickly and the sooner they could cross the roads the better. Memere and Father Louis each prayed as they walked, hoping they wouldn't see a row of truck lights in the distance.

It was two years since they ran through the night towards the protection of the priest. The children had all grown older, grew more savvy and understood a little more about what was at stake. Betty, who was now a precocious eight year old wanted to walk herself. But Cecile wouldn't let go of her. She held to the promise she made her mother and would not let go of her sister's hand. Over the hilly terrain they walked as quickly as they could. Each time the ground became flat, they ran.

They came to the last road with the church in view. In the distance, though, they saw what they dreaded. A caravan of trucks was nearing the village and they could see the Germans coming. They ran across the road and into the church.

"Lucie, you must turn around and go back now. The children will be fine with me. You must go back through the fields and get home. Please, leave now."

"All right. Come here children," she said as she bent down. "You stay with Father Louis and do exactly as he says. When the Germans leave you can come home again. This is not like before and we are not leaving you. You are just hiding here for a little while. Do you all understand?" They all did.

She kissed them in groups and quickly turned around and left.

"Come with me children. We are going to hide in the back. We are going to keep the lights off so I don't want you to be frightened." He took them to the back of the church.

Once in the rear of the sanctuary, they huddled in a small room. Father Louis sat with them and prayed they would make it through the night. He was taken by the bravery the children showed. There was no panic any longer. They all accepted what they had to do and not one of them gave him any trouble. The children slowly fell asleep as Father Louis kept a watchful eye on the church. He knew the sounds of the building and would be able to know instantly if a door opened or a window was touched. Of course, they would certainly hear a dreaded knock and he hoped that would be one sound that would not be heard.

Memere crossed the fields in a run. She was not a young woman and it was very hard to cross the fields with the speed she needed. But it would be a lot easier for her to get home on her own. She only had herself to take care of.

The Germans began to arrive in the village shortly before Memere got home. In fact she could see them pulling into the square as she got to the railroad tracks. She followed the tracks and made it back to the house. Georges was outside moving equipment and making sure there was no sign of children.

"They are safe," Memere said to Pepere.

"Who can be safe now? Not them, not us and certainly not Father Louis. This may be the night we have been dreading."

Memere and Pepere went back into the house and tried to calm down. They would have to appear normal and calm if the Germans came to their house. Would they start a search tonight? Would they wait till morning? Would the children be quiet? What if they came to the church? Could they stay hidden? There were nothing but unanswered questions.

It seemed like a long time ago when Memere and Pepere had only themselves to care for. They were never parents on their own but now their innocent, young, adopted children were in grave danger. There would be no sleeping tonight.

They quickly changed and got into their nightclothes. Everything had to be normal. Georges had gotten rid of all the straw and potato sacks and the house looked like there were no children. They waited.

The knock on their door didn't come until the afternoon of the next day. Two trucks drove up to their house and several German soldiers knocked. Pepere opened the door as Memere stirred the large pot in the chimney.

"Who lives here?" said a man with a gun.

"My wife and I live here"

"What are your names?"

A lump stuck in Memere's throat as she thought of the farmer's wife who was about to turn in Cecile and Betty.

"Georges and Lucie Boisgointier." Pepere showed him their papers.

"Have you seen any people who don't belong in the area?"

"No we haven't."

"We are looking for Jews. We know there are many hiding here. If we find any, we will arrest not only the Jews but the people who are harboring them. Do you understand?"

"We understand. There have been no Jews here. Look for yourself."

The house was so small that the Germans took a short time looking. They searched for hidden doors or false floors but with such a ramshackle house with no lights and no apparent place to hide, they were quickly satisfied they were being told the truth.

"If you discover any Jews, you must turn them in. Do you understand that?"

"Yes. Yes we will."

The Nazis turned to leave. They boarded the trucks and sped off.

Georges and Lucie looked at each other. They knew they were safe for the time being.

The Germans never came to the church to look. There were no discovered Jews in the village. The Nazis remained about two weeks and left, leaving things the way they found them—with just a few German soldiers. In that time, the children stayed huddled virtually all the time and waited for a knock that never came. Father Louis continued to bring them food and kept their spirits as high as he could.

There was a collective sigh of relief from all the villagers when the special cadre of Germans finally left their village. The Boisgointiers were safe.

Chapter Eleven

T he priest brought the children home shortly after the Nazis left the village. They were happy to see Memere again and literally burst into the front door.

"Memere, we are back home," they cried.

"We've come back to you, Memere and we are all safe."

"Oh, it's good to see all of you. Pepere and I have missed you so," she turned to the priest, "thank you so much Father Louis. I don't know how I can ever thank you. Keeping the children with you put you at so much risk. Your parishioners who all promised not to give us away took great chances as well. I wish there was something I could say."

"There's no need for that, Lucie. We are all blessed with the capacity to perform. I prefer to be thankful that I was able to do something. Besides, look at the chances you have taken. If anything, we should all look to you for inspiration."

"Look at them, Father," Memere said as the children bounced around the small room. "They would all most certainly be dead by now if we hadn't found them. I'm sure their families have all died, although we hold out some hope. They are so innocent and yet so many want them dead. I wake up every morning worried that today is the day we are going to be discovered. I have a constant vision of Nazis rounding up these children and taking them away."

"Lucie, you have made a real difference in the lives of these children. In fact you kept them alive. That will never be forgotten. Not by them, not by me and not by anyone who learns of it. Your nightmares and your visions will disappear, but your legacy will be these young ones, if we can keep them alive until this is all over."

"What happens when this is all over, Father? Things don't last forever and neither will the Nazis. Someday they will be defeated and what they've done will be a memory. What happens then? How do we live knowing what we, as humans, have been capable of doing?

"Lucie, you must look at this as a cleansing. The worst among us rise to the surface and are then destroyed. It's often unclear what true evil is. Not here. We know what the evil is and that it will sooner or later be destroyed, as evil must be."

"Well, Father, I suppose you are right. It's just so hard to think of anything good coming out of this."

Betty, Cecile and the other children settled back into life at the small house. True, there were no lights, no running water and they went to the bathroom in an outhouse. But they were with Memere and they felt loved and wanted by her. They kept to themselves, not wanting to risk anyone questioning them or turning them in. Father Louis had told everyone in his parish to care for them wherever they could, but Cecile wanted to take no chances. She and Betty stayed away from everyone.

From time to time, the little girls would walk to another village and beg for food. No one would know them and they would just be poor children without enough to eat. They always came back with something for the others. Cecile had grown wise beyond her years and she knew how to act to get people to give her food.

Pepere, once again, started to grow distant, at times going an entire day without speaking to anyone. Memere still brought the children to church from time to time, but the knowledge that everyone knew who they were and what was at stake soon became more difficult and after a while, their visits to church became rare. They lived amongst themselves, Cecile still attended school but the looks she received from the other children after the Nazi search eventually made her stop going. They were in hiding and they would stay that way.

As the months wore on, the children, in fact the entire family, grew more removed from the rest of the community. They began living a reclusive life and the children would see fewer and fewer people. In time, this caused the youngsters to close ranks among themselves and suspect anyone from outside their "family."

The boredom in and around Normandy coming from the war started to break down the discipline the family had. The children looked more and more unkempt. They spent more time in the fields and were rarely clean. They relied increasingly on themselves to make decisions and, since they were children, lacked the wisdom needed for everyday life. Without the emotional and spiritual help of an involvement in the community, their structure, whatever there was of it, started to loosen.

The toll of time, fear, undernourishment and stress had changed the children. They began to show signs of reverting to a life based on instinct. There was little intellectual stimulation and it was a struggle to get from one day to the next. Manners had fallen by the wayside. Dignity about themselves and their surroundings also broke down. Cecile had the most difficult time. She was, after all, responsible for taking care of Betty and she would never take back the promise she made to her mother. Even if she would let herself go, she still felt the need to make sure Betty was all right.

Cecile continued to tell Betty stories and to hold her hand as often as she could. They would still walk together and Cecile would tell Betty about the time when Mama, Papa and Marguerite would come for them. There were no real toys for the younger ones to play with so Cecile helped them make little toys out of wood and leaves. She made up games for them to play and generally tried to keep their spirits up. But as time wore on, even that started losing its effectiveness.

In the hottest part of a searing August afternoon, two men came to the small house. They seemed to just emerge from nowhere and walked up to the Boisgointier house. Carefully, they didn't go up to the front door but instead walked quietly around the back, where the window was. Although the window was filthy, they found a small spot which allowed them to peer into the house.

They saw poverty in its most drastic form. There was virtually no furniture. Dirt on the floor nothing on the walls. They saw children who were filthy and very few signs that they were being well cared for. The woman was extremely large and quite filthy herself. It was a very sad sight, but in this time of war and occupation, not a unique one. The men had seen worse.

The old woman was reading to them from the bible and the children were more anxious to get outside than they were to hear about God.

"All right. Go on out if you want. But bring back some more onions," Memere told them as they prepared to move out. It was so hot that they needed very little clothing. It was a good thing because they appeared to be wearing little that looked anything like clothing.

"Cecile, you mind the others."

"Yes, Memere. I'll find some big onions for the soup," the oldest said as she followed the little ones out the front door.

The men bent down and crept to the edge of the house and watched the children run out of the house and into the field. When they were deep into the field and out of sight, the two men moved to the door.

One of the men knocked on the door. There was no answer. Inside, Memere had heard the knock and froze.

He knocked a second time.

"Who is there?" Memere called out. Her voice was a bit anxious.

"Don't worry, we are friends," the man called out.

After a few moments, Memere slowly opened the door.

"Who are you?" she said as she carefully stared at the two men.

"I am Rene Auben and this is Jacques Carpontiere. We have come a long way. We are from Ouvre de Secoure Aux Enfants and we have been sent to look in on the grandchildren of the man, Mr. Widerman, who gave you Cecile and Betty."

"Oh my God," Memere said. "What is Ouvre de Secoure Aux Enfants.?"

"May we come in?" the man asked.

"Yes. Yes. Come in."

They got a close look at the misery inside the small house.

"You have suffered great deprivation, Mrs. Boisgointier," the other man said.

"We are all right. What is Ouvre de Secoure Aux Enfants?" she repeated.

"Madame, O.S.E. is an organization that cares for Jewish children in hiding from the Nazis. We have been sent from Paris to look in on these children to make sure they are being cared for in the way that their families would have wanted them to be. Their families have entrusted us to do what we can for their care."

"I have never heard of you. Mr. Widerman never told me about you," she said suspiciously.

"I can assure you that Mr. Widerman asked us to make sure the children were in good hands. He contacted us when he contacted you."

Memere continued to look at the men. She pointed to the table. "Why don't you sit down."

The men sat and Memere gave them something cool to drink.

"Mrs. Boisgointier," the first one said, "we have helped thousands of young, innocent Jews escape death at the hands of the

Nazis. We have been asked by many thousands of families to make sure their most prized possessions, their children, have an opportunity to live through this."

"Well," Memere said, "they are living through this. We all are and we will continue, with God's help, to see it at an end."

"Madam, these are Jewish children. Do they know that?"

"Of course they know that. But they don't need to know it all the time."

"But you are instructing them from the New Testament. Are you Catholic?"

"Yes, I am, but what difference does that make. We read the bible so they understand that God has a purpose, even in this miserable time. We also read the bible because it is one of the only books we have. We read the bible so we can be together as a family. What does it matter to you if we read the bible?"

"They are not clothed very well, Madame. They don't seem to have enough food. There doesn't seem to be enough food here at all, for any of you. We're concerned that their care is being compromised."

"Their care is being compromised?" Memere said, not believing what she was hearing. "Compromised? These children were at death's door. They were rescued. It has taken a great many risks to get them this far. But they live in a house of love. They are in God's hands and I won't let anything happen to them. What are you saying?"

"We don't want to be insulting. We are gratified that you are caring for these Jewish children and we can never thank you enough. But I'm just wondering whether they can receive the care we want them to receive."

The other man sought to clarify the situation. "Madame, one of the things O.S.E. does is rescue these children and take them to safe places, truly safe places. We have successfully brought more than a thousand young ones into Switzerland where they can start new lives in safety. We have not lost any yet and today, they are free of the war and can be children once again."

"Sir," Memere said with defiance, "there is no place that is safe. Not even Switzerland. I am happy that you have done your job in rescuing children. I have done mine in the same way."

"I think the Widermans would be happier to know that their children were away from here. They will be with others their age and they can be raised as Jews once more. Mrs. Boisgointier, we'd like to take them with us and arrange for their safe passage to Switzerland. We can do it. We can get them safely across the border."

"No!" Memere said angrily and quickly. "You will not take them from here. I don't know who you are, really and I could never turn these children over to you."

"They would be better off with us. They have no clothes, no schooling, no beds to sleep in and no way to keep their religious ties."

"When I agreed to take these children, it was with the understanding that I would care for them until their parents or someone from their families came to pick them up. I will not break the promise I made to their mothers, fathers and grandparents. They cry every night for their parents to come for them and with me, at least they know I am the one caring for them until that day comes." Memere didn't let the men know that Cecile and Betty had stayed with the farmer and his wife until they came within a whisker of being caught.

"Who do you think their families would be happier to see them with? A Jewish family in Lucerne or in this dirty shack in Normandy?"

"Mr. Auben, in all likelihood, their families are never coming back. I will care for them until my dying day. My vow was sacred and I will not break it."

"Madame, I must say that I cannot agree with you and I am prepared to make a full report and say you refused to allow these children to be helped. They will send other visitors who will likely take them if they look as poorly as they do today."

"If you are really sincere in wanting to rescue Jewish children, find the ones who are about to be taken away to the prisons and rescue them. I took some of these children within minutes of their being processed into the Nazi system and lost forever. And I am going to care for them, not you. You tell your organization that they are staying with the Boisgointiers, in a house filled with the love of God, love of each other and hidden from train stations or roads where Nazis can grab them. They are not going with you. That is final. Please leave my house"

The two men sat silently. They looked around a little, stared at Memere and spoke to each other in Yiddish. After a while they turned back to Memere. "You and us, we both want the same thing. We as Jews are so thankful that there are Christians such as you who are willing to risk everything for our children. This is not the best place for them in our opinion, but we cannot and will not fight with you for them. We have all made promises that we may have to pay for with our lives. A mistake and these little ones will also have to pay with theirs. But there are other children who have less care than even what you are providing. We will leave now and find them. We will take them to freedom and then we'll return for others. This will go on as long as the war continues. We wish you well and we'll see if we can provide any kind of support that will help you care for them."

The men got up and started walking to the door.

"I want to repeat myself, Mrs. Boisgointier. These are not my children but I thank you as if they were. I will pray for your safety and your ability to assure theirs. Whatever happens, the world will remember you."

Mr. Auben put out his hand and Memere shook it. They walked out the door and seemed to disappear in the same way they arrived.

When they were gone and the house became quiet once again,

Memere sat down at the table and looked around the room. She bent her head into her arms and slowly started sobbing. She cried for a long time, for herself, for the children and for their families who would be suffering far more than anyone could conceive.

O.S.E. would return to Memere two more times seeking to take the children away. The last time they came, the children were home. They screamed with fear and clutched Memere when she told them what O.S.E. wanted to do. Cecile announced that they would never leave. They left both times, believing they were right in their desire to remove the children, but unsuccessful in each attempt.

The Boisgointiers did not receive any help or support from O.S.E. during the war.

That wasn't the last visit the family would have. One day as they were sitting at the table at suppertime, there was a knock on the door. Everyone froze, as it was not the special coded knock Father Louis had. Memere got up to answer the door.

A German soldier stood in the doorway and he made Cecile's heart stop.

"What do you want? Can I help you?" Memere asked in a matter of fact way.

"I am very sorry to disturb you and your lovely family at dinnertime. I just wondered whether I might have something to eat."

The man was different from the other German soldiers they had seen. He had tears in his eyes and he looked frail—hardly the proud German soldier of the past several years.

Memere looked at him for a very long time. She finally told him to come in.

"Yes, you can join us for supper. I'll make a place for you."

"Thank you, Ma'am. I'm in your debt for this."

He sat down and looked around the table at each child. Cecile had already known the terror of soldiers at their table, having experienced the unwelcome visit of soldiers to the farmer's wife. The others just froze as the man sat staring at them.

"I saw these lovely children before as I sat on the rocks and I had hoped you would be able to show me some kindness." The man was totally defeated in body and spirit. "I have three children of my own and I have not seen them in almost four years. I miss them so much." He nearly broke down sobbing at their table.

"I have had enough of this war. I have had enough of this uniform," he angrily ran his thumb and forefinger along the lapel of his uniform. I've left my platoon and I am hiding. If I am found, I will be immediately shot, but I simply cannot do this anymore. My children should know that their father finally said 'enough' and tried to turn away from the madness."

"I'm sure they would be very proud of you," Memere said in a comforting voice. He was a young man, spoke perfect French and if not for the uniform, would look like any young man around Normandy.

"They would not be proud if their father was shot as a deserter. Or that he was in hiding from his own people."

Hiding. Now that was something Memere and the children knew about. It was so strange to feel a kinship with this soldier who, in different times, might have been responsible for some of the death and destruction the Nazis brought to France. He could have been at the train station, or peering into houses looking for hidden Jews or standing guard at the main road. Now though, the war had taken its toll on him. His eyes were hollow. He was broken.

He eagerly ate what Memere put down in front of him. The children were still frozen with fear, although Cecile was old enough to realize this soldier was different from the others. However she, too, viewed the situation with guarded suspicion.

Once he finished, he thanked Memere for the food. He even put his finger to Rene's cheek and began to cry again. He regained his composure and straightened up.

"There's one thing you should know. It won't be long until the Americans come. Some are saying that there is a chance the invasion might be here in Normandy and that it will be within the next week or so. When they come, you will be liberated and we will be killed or taken prisoner. Your years of darkness will likely soon end. Mine are just about to start. I fear I will never see my children again."

There was silence at the table for many moments. The soldier finally broke the silence as he thanked Memere again for the soup. "Years from now, please don't judge all Germans in the same way. Please see some of us with compassion and know we had the will to say 'no more'. I've got to go."

He managed a brief smile and left. His emotional speech had little effect on Cecile. She knew the uniform well and would be much happier when he was gone. She breathed a sigh of relief when he walked down past the train gates.

"Memere, what did he mean about the Americans?" Cecile asked.

"I don't know my darling. I think he meant that American soldiers will soon be coming to liberate us from the Nazis."

"Oh, how wonderful, Memere."

"Cecile, it may not be so wonderful." Memere was very concerned about what would happen. "If the Americans come there will be a terrible fight. Many people will die, including many villagers. Tomorrow we will go into the fields and build trenches so we can hide if the Americans come."

"Should we be afraid of the Americans, Memere?"

"No darling, we should be very much afraid of what will happen if they come. We could all be killed while they're trying to free us."

"We'll be careful Memere," Betty said. "We'll be very quiet when the Americans come."

"That's good Betty. That's very good. I think we should all get ready for bed now."

Memere couldn't wait for Pepere to return home. There was much to talk about now. "The Americans are coming soon," she repeated to herself over and over again. She realized that it was possible that an end to all this might be a few days away. But what if the Americans are turned back? What if there are great casualties? Could she and Pepere and the children be at risk? Probably, she thought to herself.

All the children got ready for bed with a little more excitement than usual. They had all spoken from time to time about liberation but this was the first time there was any real sign of it. Each child felt it in the air.

Memere got each of the children ready for bed and they all finally fell asleep. All except Cecile.

"If the Americans come and we are freed, can we go and look for my parents?" she wanted to know.

"Yes, darling, we can go and look for them," Memere said in an encouraging voice, even though she felt in her heart the search would be futile.

"I hope the Americans come soon, Memere. I want to see my parents and Marguerite and Grandmother and Grandfather again. When I see them I am going to hug them so tightly. They will be so surprised how Betty and I have grown. I remember all the songs we used to sing, Memere. I didn't sing them at all here because you told us not to, but I remember them and I will sing to my parents again once I find them. I hope we can find them. I hope we can."

Memere could barely hold the lump in her throat. The torch Cecile held for her parents still, remarkably, had some flame left in it. After all she had been through, all she had seen, she still carried that special warm feeling for the parents who had been brutally ripped away from her. She would willingly give up all that she had learned over the past three years just to be their little girl again. If there was only some way to head off the disappointment all these children would eventually feel. They were all told these arrangements were temporary and the children believed it. Each anticipated a joyful reunion. What could she say to them? She had to let them hold out hope.

Pepere came in after all the children were asleep and sat down to eat.

"Georges, something happened tonight that may change everything."

"What happened?"

"A German soldier, a deserter, came to the house looking for food. I gave him some and when he left, he told us that the Americans were a week or so away from arriving here."

Georges looked up with a hint of excitement, the first he had felt in months.

"This could be all over then."

"It could, if he was right. I don't know if the Americans can do it, but they are apparently ready to try. We have to take some precautions. I've told the children we have to go in the fields out back and dig some more trenches. The ones that are there now may not be big enough or deep enough if they have to stay for any length of time."

There were trenches in a lot of different places. Memere always had the children dig little holes to hide in in case Germans came. They were all covered over and difficult to spot. It was her way of staying one step ahead of their tormentors.

"Fine, we'll dig deeper holes and try to stock some of them in case there's real trouble."

"Georges. This could be the end. This could be the deliverance we've prayed for all these years."

"Let's hope we don't get killed in the crossfire."

"What do we do with the children if the Nazis are driven out? Their families are undoubtedly gone. Where will they go? "

"There will be some relative, some friend of the family still alive. We'll have to send the children back to them."

"I will hate to lose them. I've grown so attached to them. They are all so special to me. Little innocent jewels," Memere's voice choked as she spoke. "I wonder if they will have anywhere to go and anyone to care for them."

"We'll be able to go home, Lucie. To our little house with a bathroom and water and electric lights. Perhaps our lives will return to normal again."

"I don't know if I can go back. I don't know how much I will carry with me."

"Don't worry. We'll get our lives back. It will be the way it was before."

"I don't even remember what it was like before, Georges." She needed comforting after all these years. Georges wasn't going to provide it. He just stared ahead. The stress of hiding and the responsibility of all the children had left him broken far beyond his realization.

"Let's go to sleep, Lucie. I am tired."

"Me too."

Cecile and Betty went out just after dawn to close the gate for the railroad. It had been raining for days and this was the first morning they weren't pelted with raindrops when they opened the gate. They decided to walk down the tracks a little, which they often did when they didn't want to return home so quickly. They were usually the first ones up and often amused themselves for an hour until everyone was up. Hand in hand, they walked a while until they came to a bend in the tracks.

They sat in the railroad bed and waited for the train to come. Cecile still was impressed by the site of the great machine rumbling down the tracks and always waited for it. Betty liked to try to count the windows passing by. If it wasn't too fast, she could get it right.

In the distance they could hear the whine of the train. It would be a few minutes out of town but would pass by them within 10 minutes.

"Cecile, the train sounds strange," Betty said.

"What do you mean?"

"It just sounds different."

Cecile got up and went over to the tracks to feel the vibration on the tracks. There weren't any.

"That's odd," Cecile said out loud. "Where are the vibrations?"

"Maybe it's a new kind of train," Betty suggested.

"No Betty, I don't think it's a train at all." In fact, while deeply muffled, the sound was more like intermittent popping than the rythmic sound of a distant train. Within minutes, the sounds increased until all they were able to hear was the distant thunder.

Cecile stood on the tracks and stared, first into town and then turning toward the ocean. She made simulated binoculars so she could concentrate more on one spot. There in the distance she saw them. They were only specks in the distance but they were moving towards them.

"Betty, look. There are planes out there. Lots of planes. They're coming this way."

"Where? I don't see them?"

"Look, right out there. They're headed right for us."

"I see them. Maybe we should go home."

"No Betty. Let's stay for a minute and see what they're going to do."

They stayed by the railroad for another minute watching the planes move closer. It didn't take much time for the planes to be on top of them.

"Alright Betty, let's go home."

It was almost too late. The planes, which had been dropping in altitude as soon as they crossed the land line began strafing the ground in their path. Since Cecile and Betty were by the tracks, they were in the way of a strategic target. Bullets started ricocheting off the tracks as the girls ran, trying to get away.

Cecile grabbed Betty and threw her to the ground.

"Lay here and don't move," Cecile said to her sister.

They could hear the sounds of bullets and the sounds of bombs dropping in the distance. Once the first wave of planes passed by, Cecile picked Betty up and they ran towards the house. Everyone was up.

"Memere, there were planes. They were shooting at us. Is it the Americans? Is it the Americans?" Cecile kept asking.

"I don't know, but grab some of the other children and let's get away from here," Memere said excitedly.

They began to round up the children and hid them in the back, under the eaves of the house. The sound of the bombs was getting closer and the whine of airplane engines was all around them.

From the corner of the field a man came running. They couldn't make him out at first and even thought he might be a German soldier. But when he got closer they recognized Father Louis.

"Quickly, everyone, get out of the house and head for the fields near the beach. Go now," he cried. He was off, heading for the next house to warn the next family, hoping it wasn't too late.

Memere, Pepere and the children ran through the field behind the house as fast as they could. Planes were now filling the sky above them and every one seemed to be dropping bombs or firing at the panicked people running. They got to the field near the beach. There were hundreds of villagers digging holes and trenches in the rain soaked, muddied field and climbing into them for protection. Cecile and Betty found the hidden trench they had made and Cecile climbed into it.

"I don't want to go in the trench Cecile," Betty protested.

"Betty, come in the trench," said Cecile.

"It's dark in the trench and too much mud. I'm frightened."

"It will be all right. If you don't come in the trench the planes will see you and shoot you." Cecile argued.

Before Betty could say another word, Memere came up to the trench. She grabbed Betty and jumped into the hole. Pepere crawled into another hole with some of the others.

It was as loud as can be. The bombs were dropping in great

numbers and most people in the field were screaming in fright.

"What's going to happen to us Memere?" Cecile screamed.

"Just stay where you are Cecile," Memere screamed back at the frightened child. "Don't move."

Cecile held Betty's hand very tightly. Again, she remembered the promise she made to her mother.

"Don't worry, Betty. The bombs will stop soon."

"I'm scared, Cecile. What if one hits us." She had never heard such loud noises in her life. Dozens of bombs dropped around them in the first few minutes they were there. She began to scream.

"Stop it Betty, you're going to scare the others," Cecile yelled at her.

Betty stopped screaming but just stared at Cecile. She had never been yelled at like that before. Her screams became sobs.

"Oh Betty, come here. Don't be afraid." Cecile tucked her sister's head into her shoulder and held her.

More and more people were coming to the field. Some brought a little food and everyone shared what they had. The planes came in waves. Sometimes they'd stop for a while, only to begin again, with more bombs and more strafing bullets. In the distance they could hear the sounds of buildings being hit by the bombs.

They stayed there all day and all night. It was difficult for everyone but was toughest on the little ones. They grew restless staying in trenches for so long. Fortunately, early June was warm enough so they were able to make it through the night without freezing.

The second day brought still more bombs, although not as many. By now, everyone was exhausted. No one had slept much the night before.

The morning had turned to afternoon with everyone still remaining in their trenches. Betty looked out of the hole and started to scream.

"Something's coming, something's coming. Memere, look."

Memere jumped up to look. Some 25 yards away a man was crawling towards them on his stomach. He was wearing leaves on his helmet and he had on a uniform no one had ever seen before. When he got close to them he put his fingers to his lips, telling them to be quiet and to stay still.

"It's an American," Memere screamed, ignoring his order for quiet. "My God, it's an American. They've come to save us."

When the soldier got to the trench, he rolled in. He took one look at the panic on Cecile and Betty's faces and he plainly saw the joy expressed in Memere's face.

"It's all right. It's all right. We're here. You're free." He held the girls and embraced Memere.

More and more soldiers crawled into the other holes. There seemed to be thousands of them crawling up the beaches to the field. All had branches and leaves on their helmets. They had climbed up a yard at time from Utah Beach, part of the largest invasion force in history. The Americans had come, along with the British, Canadians, the rest of the Allies and, of course, the French to liberate France from the the grip of the Nazis. They landed well below the fields, at Utah, Omaha, Sword, Gold and Juno Beaches and fought their way up the bluffs and headed inland. While offically named Operation Overlord, it was more commonly known as D-Day, or "The Invasion." It would forever tie Normandy to one of the most significant events in human history.

But Cecile and Betty didn't know that then. All they knew was fear. Bombs were still exploding all around them. Bullets flew everywhere and planes continued to keep coming.

One of the bombs fell very close to the hole with Pepere and some of the other children. One of the boys, David, was hit with shrapnel and he started screaming. Memere started to jump up to go to him, the American in our hole grabbed her and pulled her back down.

"No, the boy is hurt, I must go," she said and crawled to the hole. She ripped her dress and made a bandage to cover his bleeding leg.

They stayed in the fields for another two days while a terrible battle raged around them. There were people running all over the place.

"Are you all right?" the soldier who rescued them asked.

"I want all this to stop," Cecile said.

"It will stop very soon. Don't move until all the shelling has stopped and no more soldiers can be seen. I have to keep going. Here, take some food and stay down."

"You're the first American I ever saw," Cecile said.

"Great. Then you'll always remember me. Good luck and don't move until everything has stopped. You got that girls?" he said to Cecile and Betty.

"We've got it," Betty returned.

"Okay. See you soon," he got up and headed out towards the end of the field. They never saw him again.

Finally, the bombing stopped and the planes stopped flying over. There was still smoke all over the field, but the noise had ended. It was the first time in days there was no sound of bombs or bullets. The quiet was deafening to those who were in the trenches. Slowly everyone in the field started to emerge from their holes. No one knew what to do. Everyone seemed to want to wait for someone else to leave their holes. Finally someone did. Slowly, everyone began to emerge from their trenches. Their faces were stunned, some were wounded, there was the sound of crying from some of the children and nobody was quite sure who had won the battle.

Everyone was anxious to make their way back home. They were anxious to see if there were any homes to go back to.

"Can we go home now, Memere?" Cecile wanted to know.

"Yes, we can go home. The fighting is over for now."

"Were the Germans driven away?"

Memere couldn't be sure. However in a few moments she saw several American jeeps with soldiers waving. Right then she knew.

"Georges, we're free," she cried out to her husband.

"I can see. I can see," he cried back.

"Children, the Nazis have been beaten back. The Americans have saved us!"

Memere rushed to her husband and they held each other. It was the only time Cecile had ever seen them do that.

There were screams of joy from various parts of the field as poor, frightened villagers realized they had been finally delivered from the hands of their tormentors.

As they walked, they could see the aftermath of a terrible struggle. There were bodies of Germans and Americans strewn everywhere. It was a terrible sight. Men lying dead with parts of their bodies blown away. The Americans took their dead into the church. The Germans who remained alive were all taken prisoner, so there was no one to take the bodies of their fallen soldiers anywhere. They just remained in the streets and in the fields.

Memere, Pepere and the children were dazed from the horror of the sight as they walked towards their house. For some reason, their house was not damaged at all. They walked inside and saw that nothing was broken.

"I can't believe that with all the bombs, our house is still standing," Memere said.

Everything looked the same but, of course, everything was different. No one knew quite what to do. What did liberation mean? What would happen next? Were all the Germans gone?

Everyone ran into the house to see if all their things were still intact. They were. Some things had fallen off the walls and a few of their belongings had spilled onto the ground. Cecile immediately ran for her hiding spot to see if her bag of memories and her doll were okay. She was relieved to find everything in order. Memere looked around for the animals, who must have been desperately frightened by the shelling. Finally, the dog emerged from behind a chair which had fallen down. When he saw the family he jumped out, throwing himself on Memere and licking and playing with each of the children.

Memere started to prepare some soup as the children and Pepere were quite hungry. They had been in the fields for four days.

Cecile took the dog and walked outside. She went towards the tracks to see if any part of them were damaged. She saw a man lying next to the gate. He was dead, but Cecile could not keep her eyes off him. She sat down and just stared at him. He looked about nineteen years old with very blond hair and white skin. His blue eyes were wide open, staring blankly to nowhere. His hair was full of dried caked blood, his own no doubt. He must have been hit in the back of the head. The dried blood covered his nose and mouth too. His rifle was lying in the mud just a few feet away.

Cecile was drawn to the young, dead soldier. At that moment, she did not see a German uniform, just a young man lying dead near the railroad tracks. But he was a German and the more she looked at him, the angrier she got. She stared at him intently wondering how he died, whether he was in pain at the end, and whether he saw his end coming.

Cecile sat there for nearly an hour, getting more furious at him as the time passed. She wanted to yell at him, to tell him what the Germans did to her family. She wanted him to know that her family was gone and maybe they'll never return. She felt the need to yell at him and tell him she was frightened at the farmer's house and was scared to death walking to the priest's house. She was glad he was dead and hoped all his friends were killed too.

She began to curse the soldier, even though he was still and already cold. With a growing fury, she stood up and walked over to where his gun was lying. She picked up his rifle and felt it in her hand. She determined how to point it and found the firing mechanism. She wanted to shoot him again and again, for Mama, for Papa, for Marguerite and for everyone else who was hurt by the Germans. She pointed the gun at him. She saw his face in her aim and was prepared to fire at him.

Suddenly, Memere came running out of the house.

"Cecile, what are you doing? Put the gun down. Cecile, put the gun down."

"I want to kill him Memere. I'm going to kill him—with his own gun."

"Put it down." Cecile finally lowered the rifle. Memere came and sat down next to Cecile.

"Cecile, darling, he's already dead. The Americans killed him and all the others. They can't hurt us anymore. They can't hurt you and Betty anymore. Let's go back to the house now."

"I don't want to Memere. I want to shoot him."

"Well you can't stay here all night staring at this dead soldier. He's already dead. He can't be killed twice. Someone did it for you."

"I can't seem to walk away. He doesn't look like a soldier now. He's just a dead young man. I hope his family is worried about where he is."

"I'm sure they are and it will be very sad when they find he is dead. They will wish he never became a soldier and will wish he was still a little boy. But we can't change any of that for him."

"I'm glad he won't ever have children of his own, or see his wedding day," Cecile began to cry.

"That's fine, darling. But because of what the Americans did in the past few days, you will. There was a horrible fight here, my darling. But it's over now. We don't have to worry about the Germans any more and we must try to find a way to go back to the way we were before."

"Can I go to Paris and look for my parents?"

"Yes darling. As soon as we know what we are permitted to do, we'll go to Paris and try to find out what happened to your family."

Cecile slowly got up. She started to walk away, but turned around. She bent over and spat at the dead soldier.

"Good for you," she yelled. "Good for you." Over the next few days, Cecile saw many bodies. When they were German, she spat at them the same way she spat at the one near her house. When they were American, she would pick up flowers and gently place them on the body of the soldier. The enormity of what took place in her little community started to sink in to Cecile very soon after the battle ended.

Memere took her by the hand and they walked toward the house. Cecile looked back at the dead man once. He was still there. But then she bounded into the house to the other children and to their first day of liberation.

MOMMY, DADDY, PLEASE DON'T LEAVE ME.
THE BABY IS CRYING, PICK HER UP.
WHY ARE ALL THESE PEOPLE BEING PUSHED INTO THE TRAIN
MOMMY, DADDY, I DON'T LIKE THE GERMANS, THEY ARE HURTING
THE CHILDREN. THE TRAIN IS LEAVING, PLEASE DON'T LEAVE ME.
I AM SCARED, I DON'T WANT TO GO.
STAY WITH ME.
MOMMY, DADDY, WHY ARE WE BEING HURT.
BABY, PLEASE DON'T CRY. I'LL TAKE CARE OF YOU.
MOMMY AND DADDY ARE NOT HERE ANYMORE.
THE GERMANS TOOK THEM AWAY.
DON'T CRY BABY. I WON'T LEAVE YOU.
MOMMY, DADDY, WHERE ARE YOU.
PLEASE DON'T LEAVE ME.

Poem by
Cecile
Widerman,
1945

Cecile
Widerman
at the
orphanage
in 1946.

Cecile's older sister,
Marguerite Widerman.

Cecile's mother and father, Laja and Herz Widerman.

Betty Widerman. The youngest of the girls. She was only six the night the Nazis stormed their neighborhood.

Cecile and Marguerite always had a special bond between them. Although there was a seven year difference in age, Cecile was quite attached to her older sister and forever wanted to be like her.

Herz in a quiet moment at a local Parisian park.

Memere, Pepere and all the children lived in this small house in Normandy. They were responsible for maintaining the railroad gate, which allowed trains to pass through toward and away from the town.

Marguerite Widerman. The oldest of the Widerman sisters. She was engaged to be married to Henri when Paris was overrun and occupied by Germany.

The Star of David that Jews across Europe were forced to wear as a badge of degradation and identification. The entire Widerman family wore the Star after the Nazis occupied France. For Cecile, it became a lifetime symbol of connection with her lost family.

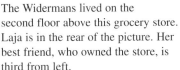

The Widermans lived on the second floor above this grocery store. Laja is in the rear of the picture. Her best friend, who owned the store, is third from left.

Marguerite, Herz and Cecile in 1934. The photo was originally captioned in Hebrew, however Memere erased the lettering while Cecile and Betty were hiding in Normandy to prevent the Nazis from discovering they were Jews.

Papa, Marguerite, Cecile and Mama in a Paris park in 1935.

The extended Widerman family at the same outing in a park in Paris in 1935. Laja and Herz are at the right, Cecile in the center of the middle row and Marguerite is in the center of the first row.

Shortly before the Nazis invaded their neighborhood, Cecile received a little pocketbook for her birthday. As the soldiers entered her apartment, Cecile placed as many meaningful items as she could into the pocketbook and carried it with her for the next five years. It is truly the chronicle of her youth.

Heroism is found in many corners and sacrifice is often borne by those with no apparent cause. Memere, Pepere and Father Louis shared a bond of courage that went far beyond what could have been expected of them. They gambled everything, including their lives, to hide a group of young Jewish children, alone and on the run from history's most terrible evil.

Father Louis in 1963.

Memere, Pepere and young Rene, one of the hidden children, shortly after the war.

Betty, far left and Cecile, second from left, visiting Father Louis during their return to Paris in 1963, in part to determine the fate of their family.

NE MOUBLIEZ PAS

FORGET ME NOT

NO MOLVIDES

VERGISS MICH NICHT

CÉCILE

The number of Jewish children who lost their parents during the Nazi occupation of France was so large, that it is almost impossible to determine accurately. The nine children here (Cecile is in the back row at far right) with two of the staff who cared for them bore the scars of that time and were the youngest victims of the Holocaust.

A going away card presented to Cecile as she prepared to leave the orphanage. While the other children envied her new life in America, they already understood the pain of separation.

Chapter Twelve

There were American soldiers all around. They seemed pleasant and enjoyed being seen as heroes. To everyone in Normandy, they were the liberators. Since the Boisgointiers had no radio and read no newspapers, they were behind the times in terms of what happened in the war. The American soldiers told the villagers a little about what had happened on the battlefields of World War II

But they all left one thing out, no one talked about Hitler's Final Solution and what had happened to more than six million Jews.

Life didn't change much for anyone in the village, although a great tension was lifted. The constant fear was gone, especially for the Boisgointiers. The terror that a German soldier would find them ended with the row of German prisoners being marched toward the train station and even more with the row after row of bodies that were lined up outside the church.

Still, the problem of getting enough to eat was the same as it had always been. But the children knew how to beg for food from the soldiers and almost always came away with something.

Cecile was closing the gate one morning when an American

soldier came by. He took off his cap and waved to her. She gave a brief, hesitant wave back.

"Do you always open the gate yourself?" the soldier asked in English, attempting some conversation.

Cecile pointed to her ears and shook her head, indicating she could not understand the English the man was speaking.

He then asked her in French if she spoke German. Cecile said she didn't but said she could speak Yiddish. The man's eyes lit up. He hadn't spoken Yiddish in quite some time. He introduced himself to Cecile in Yiddish, saying his friends all called him Katz. He reached out his hand to shake the girl's.

"My name is Cecile," she responded in Yiddish, also one of the few times she had spoken the language in several years. She shook his hand tentatively.

"Do you open the gate yourself every day?" he asked in Yiddish.

"Yes. It's my job."

"It looks like a tough job for a young girl. How old are you."

"14."

"Hey are you hungry? How about your family? Are they hungry?"

"We never have enough to eat."

"Well, I've got some cans of food. Bring them to your family." He pulled out a stack of cans from his backpack and laid them out on the ground.

Cecile never saw canned food before and didn't quite know what to make of it. Katz opened the cans and Cecile reached in and started to eat from one.

"No, not that one," Katz said, pulling it away. "That's for your dog."

Cecile grabbed it back from Katz and ate it anyway. The soldier just looked at her and smiled. She was 14 but she looked no more than eight, he thought. Undernourished, frightened all the time, hardly a way for a child to spend her youth.

"Well, I've got to go. I'll come back and visit you again and I'll bring more food for you and your family. We'll talk more in Yiddish, too. Good-bye Cecile. You take care of yourself, okay?"

"Good-bye Katz," she said almost in a whisper.

After the liberation, Memere, Pepere and all the children could walk into the village without worrying any longer about being caught. There was no more running away, no more German soldiers—just Americans and they did not have to run away from them.

When they walked into the village, they would see women with their heads shaved.

"What happened to those women, Memere. Why are their heads shaved?"

"Those women went with the German soldiers," she said with sadness. On occasion, people would throw stones at them and would call them names. Many of them were put in jail, but all were marked for life. Had the Germans won, they might have been among the few who were treated well. However since the Germans were defeated, these women were now hated and pitied by their own.

Katz came over often. He would always bring food with him and he would always have a lot of pleasant conversation for Cecile. He became a father figure to her. It was obvious the girl needed a lot of affection and after her long ordeal she would only slowly begin to emerge from her emotional prison. Betty would climb onto Katz's lap and the three of them would sing songs. He would tell them of America and they would tell him of Paris during better times. He would take them for rides in his jeep and the girls would laugh and giggle throughout the entire ride.

During one of his visits, Cecile asked Katz if he could help her.

"What would you like me to do?" the soldier said.

"Could you find out for me if my parents and my grandparents are back in Paris?" She gave him a little note with their addresses on it. He looked at the note and then stared at the young girl. He realized that she had no idea about what had happened to Jews all across Europe. She had no idea of the long train rides, the gas chambers or the crematoria.

"I will look into it for you Cecile," he said tenderly. "I don't know what I can do, but I'll ask someone to see what they can find out."

"Oh, I hope you can find them. I can't wait to see them again."

Cecile asked Katz about her parents every time they saw each other, but he never gave her an answer. He already knew the answer but he couldn't bear being the one to tell Cecile what probably happened to them.

One of the notable things right after the liberation was the increase in traffic on every road. In the past, there would be an occasional vehicle on the road in front of the house. Now, there was one almost every minute. Each time a car or truck would drive by, the Boisgointier's dog would run out and bark at it. Cecile was frightened each time the dog would go out into the street because he would get so close to the wheels. She was always so relieved when he came bounding back towards the house.

Then, it happened. He had jumped out into the street after a truck and had been run over by its back wheels.

Cecile watched the horror from the house and went running out into the street. The truck never stopped. The dog was alive but very badly injured. She bent down to the dog and pleaded with it not to die.

"Don't go away from me. Please you silly dog, don't die. Not yet."

She cradled the dog's head in her arms and rocked back and forth. It was too late, he died right there in the road. Cecile sat in the road alone with the dog for a moments. She was angry. Angry at the truck driver, angry at the all the soldiers, even angry at the dog. She didn't know what to do. She just let her anger and her grief spill out of her. She finally picked the poor animal up and carried him to the front door. She gently laid him down in the garden and went in to tell Memere.

Memere was as upset as Cecile. The dog, after all, had been with them for years. He had been hidden with them and been liberated with them. Now, just after the best days in their lives, their wonderful dog was taken from them. Memere and the children dug a hole and buried the dog after a short, sad ceremony.

After that, the only thing that made Cecile feel better was her visits with Katz. There were no more Germans but life hadn't seemed to get much better, except when Katz came by. He reminded her of her Papa and she waited for the time they spent together. They would laugh and sing and tell more and more stories, most of which were made up. It was her favorite time.

Only a few weeks after the liberation, Katz came by with some happy news for Katz, but very bad news for Cecile. Since the fighting had ended where they were, the army was sending him back home to his family. He would be leaving right away.

"Why do you have to go?" Cecile asked sadly.

"Everything we came to do here has been done. Normandy is free, the Germans are gone and now we must start to rebuild our lives--all of us."

"But I don't want you to go, Katz. Can Betty and I go with you?"

"No Cecile, you can't. I'm sorry. I will write you all the time though and tell you more stories about the USA. Maybe one day you'll come there."

Cecile said she'd wait for his letters but a very lonely feeling came over her. Once again she was to be separated from someone she cared deeply about, just as she needed him most. Cecile cherished his love, friendship and security, but now he was leaving her and she couldn't understand why.

They said good-bye in front of the house. He embraced Memere, shook Pepere's hand and kissed each child. When he kissed Cecile, the young girl wouldn't let go. Memere had to pull her away from the soldier. He waved as he walked down the road. All the children waved until he was out of sight. Cecile stayed and waved some more.

After Katz left, the family's daily routine continued. Other soldiers came by on a regular basis. Each dropped off some food. Some of them said they were friends of Katz, others just seemed to enjoy the children. Life hadn't changed all that much in Normandy. But at least there were no more Germans.

Early in the fall a large car pulled up in front of Memere's house. A well dressed couple stepped out and looked around. They came to the house and asked Memere about Betty and Cecile. The woman told Memere she was the children's Aunt Helene. A soldier friend of Katz' had found her and told her where the children were.

"I'm so happy to find they are well," Aunt Helene said. "My parents were smart to let you care for them."

"Thank you," Memere said guardedly. "They are wonderful children and we are all a very happy family."

"Well, that's nice to hear," she said as she lit a cigarette. "But I'm here to take them back to Paris."

"You're what?"

"I'm taking them with me back to Paris. The Germans are gone and they belong back in the city where they grew up."

"But you can't take them now," Memere protested. "They've been through so much. They need time to recover from a very horrible ordeal. I think it would be better if you waited a few more months."

"Well, I appreciate your concern, but I am their aunt and I am going to take them back to Paris."

Cecile and Betty came out into the room, showing a mixture of joy and sadness. It was a few years since they had seen her and while she did represent the family they yearned for, both girls felt a little strange in her presence.

"Hello children. How about a kiss for your favorite aunt?"

The girls came over and gave the woman a kiss on the cheek. It was hardly a kiss reserved for a favorite aunt.

"Girls," Memere said. "Your aunt wants to take you back to Paris with her."

"We don't want to go back to Paris with her," Betty objected.

"We want to back to Paris with you, Memere. Like we said," Cecile added.

"Nonsense," the aunt said. "I'm your aunt and your parents would much prefer you to be with your own flesh and blood."

"Please," Memere said "I made a promise to their grandparents that I would be responsible for them. That I would take care of them. They are just not ready to go back yet."

"Well, your responsibility has ended. I am their aunt and they will be returning to Paris with us."

"Alright," Memere said, resigned to their fate. "Children, let's get your belongings together and get you ready to go back to Paris."

"Do we have to, Memere?"

"I'm afraid you do."

"Will you be able to visit us?" Betty asked.

"You can bet I will never be far away from you. You were always able to find me in the past and it will be the same way in the future."

"But we don't want to leave." Betty protested.

"That's only right because I don't want you to leave either. But she is your aunt and I am afraid family has rights." She turned to the aunt angrily. "I could take you to court, you know, and we would win."

Aunt Helene laughed at Memere as she looked around the room. "I can see by your lovely home that you have plenty of extra money to spend in court. With all the children left with no families, any court would be happy to reunite a child with its lost relatives."

Memere realized Helene was probably right. There was silence in the room as Memere thought about what to do. The other children just stared at the aunt like she was a cat threatening a nest of just hatched birds. "We'll run away and come back here," Cecile threatened, breaking the silence.

"Don't do that Cecile. There would be no point. Look, sit down next to me." The two girls huddled right by her side. "We have been through so much together, haven't we? Look at what we have seen. Look at the close calls we have been through and look at how we survived. You must take all of that and use that to create a new life for yourselves. I've learned a lot from you two. I am a much better person because I had a chance to know you. I suppose it's easier if it happens quickly, without any warning. You'd have to go sooner or later. Now I want you to put away your tears and do what your aunt says."

"We'll do it only because you say it's all right," Betty said defiantly.

"Well then, that's enough for now. No tears."

They walked into the other room where their Aunt Helene and her boyfriend were waiting impatiently.

"Are you ready girls? It's time for us to go. Well, I want to thank you for caring for the girls and I hope they weren't too much trouble."

"They were no trouble. I would die for these girls. I hope you feel the same."

Aunt Helene glared at Memere as her boyfriend picked up the girls' belongings and took them out to the car. Cecile and Betty gave each child a hug and a kiss. They kissed Pepere and said a long good-bye to Memere, who said, under her breath, "no tears, no tears." Memere broke the embrace and led the girls into the back seat of the car. The girls got settled in the open car and turned to wave to Memere and Pepere and the children. Memere held a handkerchief to her mouth as the car rolled down the road. Aunt Helene and her boyfriend never looked back. Cecile wondered who would now close the gates when the train came. In an instant, they were gone.

Cecile and Betty's return to Paris was anything but triumphant. They were very uneasy about what they would find in the city. They hadn't been in Paris for more than two and a half years and the world had changed in that time. The last time they saw Paris was agony for them and their memories of the time before that were quite fogged, especially for Betty. But the cleansing that had taken place with the chasing of the Nazis was less apparent than how to recover from the horrors they had created.

Aunt Helene and her boyfriend lived in a one room apartment on the other side of the city from where the girls had lived. The place was small with a dank, dark smell and Cecile, Betty, Aunt Helene and her boyfriend, Martin slept in the same bed.

The girls hated this arrangement. At least at Memere's they had their own little space, even if it was just a sack on the floor. They both cried themselves to sleep the first night, Cecile holding her sister close the entire time.

From the time they returned to Paris, Aunt Helene paid little attention to the girls. She would go out most of the time and left the girls alone. For the first few days, Cecile and Betty wandered the boulevards near the apartment trying to see what the city had become.

It was not the same city as before. Everyone seemed to look sad. Even though liberation was still fresh in the air, the reality of living day to day made the city a dark place. There was little being done, although Paris was tooling up for a return to French industry and commerce. Many people wandered the streets, looking for work, looking for food, looking for family members. Cecile was uncomfortable in the streets, she still carried the bitter memories of Parisians screaming at them that they were dirty Jews and deserved to die. How could she look at these people again?

The most pressing thing on Betty and Cecile's minds was finding food. They begged at restaurants and even knocked on doors for something to eat. They eeked out enough for a meal here and there but begging was difficult in a city where begging was all around them.

Eventually, Aunt Helene told Cecile that she was to go to work in a factory. She was to give all the money she made to Aunt Helene in exchange for the room and board she provided. Every morning, 14-year-old Cecile got up and went to work and struggled through the door at night. At the end of each week, Cecile gave her salary to her aunt who took it to help finance her social life. While Cecile was working, Betty stayed with Aunt Helene's friends. Neither of the girls was allowed to go to school.

Since Betty and Cecile had no parents to care for them, the French government made money available to them. Aunt Helene took that money as well. Fortunately, when Cecile went to the office to sign the papers giving Aunt Helene the money from the government, she was told of an organization catering to people who lost everything to the Nazis. If not for that organization, the children may have starved.

Weeks went by and Cecile and Betty grew increasingly depressed. When she wasn't working, Cecile was wandering the streets of Paris with her sister in tow. They would pass bakeries with wonderful smells and Cecile knew that it would be easy to go in and take some food when no one was looking. But she remembered Memere telling her that she was never to take anything that didn't belong to her, so they just continued on. Memere wrote to the girls often but receiving the letters just made the girls feel worse. How they wished they could go back to Memere.

They wandered through the city day after day, at least when Cecile didn't have to go to work. Like many others who were displaced and afraid, they discovered the look of the new Paris. The city was struggling so hard to return to some sense of normalcy, there was no room for compassion for two little girls. So they continued to drift, in and out of neighborhoods they knew. Up and down streets that were clearly as well as vaguely familiar. But all the while the yearning for what once was guided their days and nights.

They had just passed a restaurant and watched for a while as people ate their lunch outside when they saw him. At first Cecile just stared at the man. She thought she recognized him. She followed him a little while just to make sure it was him. It was.

As they passed the cafeteria, she dropped Betty off with one of the women who worked there. She continued to follow the old man. Cecile was sure he was with the group that was taken from their home that horrible July night.

When the man reached the corner he turned around abruptly. Cecile was too close. The man was able to stare into her face and she into his. There was nothing in his eyes at first, he stared blankly at her, or through her would be more accurate. But as he looked at her little face, his eyes seemed to soften and the tightness around his mouth loosened. He bent down almost to her height and then slowly began to weep. Cecile started to cry as well, but soon the man was almost inconsolable. His tears flowed like rain and he bent lower and lower until he was kneeling on the sidewalk.

"You are Cecile. You are Laja and Herz' little girl. The middle one."

"Yes! I'm Cecile," she cried.

"You are alone. I know you are alone. Everyone is gone," he said.

"Yes. We have been away for so long. I'm looking for someone we know. Anyone. Everything has changed," Cecile said.

"Everything has changed. You're right. You've been away and I have been away too. They took me away with my family and now I'm the only one who has come back."

"My sister and I are the only ones who've come back, too. Except for my aunt. She's here too."

"Poor little girls. All alone."

"Do you know what happened to my parents and to my sister Marguerite?"

The man stared at her for a long while. His face changed many times as he stared at her.

"Cecile. I must tell you something. Come here." Cecile came closer and sat on the sidewalk with him. "Cecile. Your father. He is alive. He is near here. I saw him no more than two months ago."

"What!" she cried. "Papa is alive. Oh my god. Where is he. Where is Mama and Marguerite?"

"I don't know about them. I only saw your father. He was sick in the hospital."

"What hospital? Where? Please tell me."

"It is outside the city. You can get there by the train. It's in Drancy. You take the train and when you get off it's right on the other side of the market. A two story building. You can't miss it."

Cecile was shaking as she tried to make sure she'd remember. "Can you take me there?"

"No. I can never go back there. But your Papa. He's there. You'll be with your Papa again, my little one. You'll be with your Papa."

"I don't have any money. How can I get on the train?"

"Someone will give you the money. You'll be able to go. But go now. Your Papa is waiting. He's asked for you many times."

"Oh thank you," Cecile sobbed. "Thank you, thank you. I can't wait to see my Papa."

The man stood up and looked at her. A poor little girl on the pavement. "I've got to go. Don't forget. Drancy, right behind the market." He turned around and continued walking down the street.

Cecile immediately turned around and ran toward the train station. She didn't stop at street corners and almost knocked into the people slowly walking down the street.

"I'm going to see Papa. I'm going to see Papa," she cried both to herself and out loud.

Cecile got to the train station and ran to the ticket counter. "When is a train to Drancy?" she asked the man.

"There is one in about 15 minutes. Do you need a ticket, young lady?"

"No. I just want to know when it arrives."

She walked to the end of the station. When the train came in she would get on and hope the conductor would some how overlook her or let her on for free.

Fifteen minutes later, Cecile saw the light from the train. It grew brighter as it came lazily around the bend into the station. Once it stopped people began to get off while others who were in the station climbed aboard. Cecile climbed onto the last car and looked for a place to sit down. There were others in the car, which was perhaps half full. She slunk down into the seat and waited for it to pull out of the station. She could hear the hissing and then she felt the gentle but obvious jolt as it started to pull out. Soon she'd be with Papa and all this nightmare would be over. Then they'd look for Mama and Marguerite. Papa would know where to look. He'd know who to talk to.

The conductor made his way down the cars and Cecile could see him entering the car. He stopped by each person who got on and took their ticket. When he got to her he asked for her ticket.

"I am only going to Drancy, sir. I don't have a ticket and I don't have any money for one. I am going to find my Papa in the hospital."

The conductor bent down to talk to her. "Everyone has to have a ticket, miss." Cecile, frightened but determined, stared right at him. He could throw her off the train at any moment. She knew that. But maybe he would be kind and let her stay.

"I'll tell you what," the conductor said with a hint of a smile. "Drancy is not far away and you'll be my guest on my train today." The conductor then took a ticket from his pocket and gave it to her. "This is if you need to come back."

"Thank you," Cecile said over and over again. She was so

relieved and knew that at least she had a ticket back. Papa would find a way to get on the train. If she had to, she'd give Papa her ticket.

Cecile watched the streets go by. It was a stark contrast to the past few times she was on a train. There was no fear this time, only the most agonizing anticipation. She wished it would go much faster.

After what seemed like an eternity, the conductor called out the next few stops and Drancy was second. It wouldn't be long now. A short stop at a desolate kind of station brought few new passengers on board and almost no one got off. After a few moments the train started to pull out. The next stop would be hers. She began to stretch her neck to see out the window. She looked for something that looked like a two story hospital or any sign of a market.

They began to get close and the conductor called out Drancy. Cecile still couldn't see any landmark that would let her know where she was. She got up and moved toward the door. At least it was still daytime. She wasn't afraid but knew she still would have to be careful. All the while she looked out the windows as she walked toward the door.

The train pulled into the station and slowed and finally came to a stop. She could barely contain her excitement. The people in front of her moved down the three stairs and when she got to the bottom she had to jump onto the platform. But there she was. She would soon be with her beloved Papa.

Once on the platform she looked around, trying to decide which way she had to go. The train began to pull out of the station and soon the people leaving had thinned out the platform. Cecile stayed on the platform, looking in all directions. She saw no sign of a market. There was no gray two story building either, but she knew it had to be there. The man said it would be there.

She left the station and walked out into the street. It was an isolated location, not like in Paris. But there were no buildings of any kind. The station was in the middle of a large field. It was filled with all kinds of junk and there were very few people walking on the streets. Cecile began to get very scared. She didn't know where she was and what she came for didn't seem to be anywhere in sight. She walked along the tracks in the hope of finding a policeman or a soldier or anyone.

It felt like a long time until she came to row of shops. In front of one of the shops was a policeman. "Oh thank God," she thought. She ran to him.

"Excuse me sir, could you tell me where the hospital is."

The policeman bent down to listen to her. "I'm sorry, miss. What did you say?"

"Where is the hospital? I'm here to find my Papa. His friend said he was in the hospital behind the market and now I can't find it," Cecile began to cry.

The policeman looked at her for a moment and then bent down further, just like the man from her neighborhood did just a few hours before.

"I'm sorry to tell you this sweetheart, but there is no hospital in Drancy. Anyone who is sick goes to St. Mere, but that's 10 kilometers from here. Who told you there was a hospital here?"

"A man who knew my parents in Paris. He said he saw my Papa in Drancy. He said he was in hospital here. It was right behind the market. I'd see it as soon as I got off the train. I just got off the train and couldn't find it."

The policeman looked at her ruefully. "There is no hospital in this village at all. And this is the only market that's left," he said, pointing to the small market among the stores in the row. "I'm afraid that someone has told you a terrible story. Do you know who this man was?"

"Yes. He was a friend of my Papa and Mama. He said he was taken away and was the only one to come back, just like me. He said he saw Papa in a hospital here." Cecile's tears streamed down her cheeks and she could barely finish the story.

"I think the man was terrible for lying to you. It sounds like he was crazy. Probably from being away himself. I'm very sorry."

Cecile stepped back and brought her hands to her mouth. The man had lied to her. He never saw Papa. Why would he say that? Why would he do that to her?

"Do you need any help, miss? Do you know anyone else in Drancy?" the policeman asked. Cecile just shook her head. She couldn't even answer.

"I'll take you back to the station if you'd like."

Cecile just walked backwards, away from the policeman. The agony in her heart was clear on her face. When she got far enough away from him she turned and ran. She ran as hard as she could. She was running towards the station and crying aloud all the way there. She couldn't catch her breath and she couldn't get herself to calm down.

She was crushed by the disappointment of losing her Papa a second time and fueled by rage at the lie the man had told her. She would find him and tell him how horrible a man he was. Maybe more. She stood against the wall of the train station and just slowly sunk to the ground. She buried her little head in her hands and waited for the train to come back. Now she'd need that ticket.

Once on the train, she was in the last car again. As it pulled out of the station she looked through the back window. All there was was a big field. Nothing else. There was no hospital. There was no market. And worst of all, worse than anything, there was no Papa.

While Cecile's pain was enormous, in a short time she began to think about her sister. Betty didn't know where Cecile was and would probably be worried. It was late in the day and the first sign of dusk was apparent. It would be dark soon and Betty would be hungry and worried about what to eat. Cecile's devastating blow had begun to give way to the concern for her sister. That's just what her Mama would have wanted.

Cecile got off the train in Paris and went back to the cafeteria to get Betty. She found her sister having supper and laughing with two other children and one of the directors. They all asked where Cecile was and she told them she was just out walking. That's all she was doing. Just walking.

For the next few days, Cecile tried to find the man who told her the story about her Papa. But she never saw the man again. He was left to the delusions created for him by the insanity of the past five years.

One day Cecile left Betty at the cafeteria and went back up to the apartment. She opened the door and was shocked by what she saw. Nearly a dozen people were all taking drugs and having sex. Aunt Helene jumped up and started to yell at Cecile that she had no business returning unannounced. But Cecile didn't let her finish. She picked up her little bag of memories and walked out of the apartment.

Cecile took Betty to the director of the organization. He told them of an orphanage near Paris with children who had lost their families in concentration camps. While Betty and Cecile had no proof they were orphans, Cecile felt it was their best chance to get fed and be with people who cared for them.

A man who worked at the organization went with Cecile back to Aunt Helene's apartment. Cecile opened the door. The events of earlier in the day had ended.

"I want to say one thing and I don't want you to say anything," the man said to Aunt Helene. "I am taking the children out of here and bringing them to an orphanage where they will be cared for. If you say anything, if you object in any way, I will go right to the authorities and tell them what happened here today and about how you've prevented these girls from going to school and made a 14-year-old girl go to work. Now you just stay in your chair and we will leave. Cecile wanted to show you the courtesy of letting you know she was all right."

Aunt Helene never moved from her chair. She never said a word. Cecile and the man walked out of the apartment and out of

Aunt Helene's life forever.

The girls were taken to a large, beautiful house with a big yard. The house had been donated by wealthy Jews who had escaped from the Nazis. They were introduced to the director and the 30 other children. Everyone seemed nice enough.

After a walk around the grounds, the director suggested the girls take a shower. Neither Cecile nor Betty had ever seen a shower before and had to be taught how to use one.

After the shower, they were given clean clothes and a hot meal. They were assigned to bedrooms. Both girls were given roommates their own age. At first it was unnerving for both girls to be sleeping away from each other, even if was just down the hall, but it was nice to be with other girls their own ages. It was even nicer to have clean sheets and a real bed to themselves.

Cecile and Betty were happy for the first time in a long time. If it were not for the constant wondering about their parents, they would have been completely relaxed. The orphanage was trying to find out what had happened to the parents of the children but were not able to find any sign of what happened to them.

There were thousands of children throughout France who were alone and many orphanages began to open up. They were financed in part by the French government. But they were kept afloat by the remaining Jews in France and by Americans. The girls truly had a new life. They went on trips, played games, attended school and were fed well.

Each child in the orphanage received mail from Americans who were given their names by various organizations. Cecile received letters from a man named Max who lived in a place called the Bronx. He and his wife regularly sent them food and clothing.

Betty received a letter from a doctor living outside New York City. She asked Cecile to write the doctor back thanking him for his letter. They began a relationship by mail and the doctor constantly sent the children gifts, including money and food.

After several months at the orphanage Cecile received a special letter from the doctor. He said that since he and his wife had no children of their own they would love to have Cecile and Betty come live with them in America. Cecile held her breath. "America" she thought to herself. How wonderful that would be.

Cecile burst into Betty's room.

"Betty, the doctor wants to know if we would come to America and live with them. America!"

"America!" Betty cried out. "We can go to America?"

"How lucky we are. We'll be together and we'll live in America."

The girls experienced a wave of joy. The wave was short-lived as they both thought about what they'd be leaving behind.

"Cecile, how can we go without knowing about Mama and Papa and Marguerite?"

"I suppose we can't. Unless we know for sure that they aren't coming back, we can't go anywhere. I'm sure if they are alive, they are waiting for us and we have to do the same."

"Can we go to our apartment and see if they are there? Maybe someone in the building saw them."

"I'll tell you what Betty, we'll go to the apartment and see. If they are there or we can find anything out we'll stay in Paris. If we can't, we'll go to America and leave word for Mama and Papa where we are."

"Good. Can we go tomorrow?"

"We'll see."

First Cecile wrote to the doctor telling him they'd be very happy to come to America to live with them if they could not find their parents. He wrote back telling the girls that he would have his friend, Mr. Green, come by to look in on them. Mr. Green was a friendly man who always brought gifts for them when he visited.

It took a long time, several months, for the papers allowing them to leave France to be finalized. But when that day came, and they were told they could join the doctor in America if they wanted, Cecile knew they would have to go back to where they lived, once and for all. She had both looked forward and dreaded this day for so long. She had held out hope for her parents for so long, even while they were in the orphanage. The hope that her parents would find them after being told where they were was the thread that kept the girls together. Now, she would face the moment of truth. She would have to walk back into the horrors of her past and relive the moments that changed her life forever.

The director of the orphanage drove them to their old neighborhood. As the car slowly drove down the streets of what was once their home, Cecile became very upset. The reality that their parents may not be there was sinking in. Worse, the likelihood they were dead was there, too.

The car stopped in front of their building. The director asked if the girls wanted her to come with them.

"No, we can do it," Cecile said. "Come on Betty."

The two girls left the car and slowly walked up the stairs. Cecile remembered what it was like the last time they were on those stairs. She remembered the pain and anguish of that day. She thought of the angry Germans in uniform and the jeering people on the sidelines.

Cecile and Betty walked up the inside stairs to their apartment. There were special locks on the doors of all Jewish apartments, put there by the Nazis, so no one could get in. However, the Germans removed the normal locks and it was easy to see inside the apartments. Cecile walked to her front door and knocked. "Please answer" she said to herself.

"I don't hear anything, Cecile. Do you?" Betty said.

"No, I don't hear anything either."

"Knock again." Cecile knocked a second time, but the stillness didn't change.

"Look in the hole, maybe they were there."

Cecile pulled the garbage out of the hole and looked inside.

The apartment was exactly the same as it had been when they were taken away. Cecile could see the newspaper on the coffee table. Her Papa probably read it the night before the Nazis came. She could see the kitchen and recognized the old dishes her parents had. Cecile was even able to see a corner of their room. Her bed was unmade, witness to the brutal awakening they had that terrible night. She could see her parents clothing hanging on the wall, her papa's jacket and her mama's coat. They hadn't been moved for years.

"What do you see Cecile?" Betty asked.

"There's nothing here, Betty," Cecile said sadly. "They haven't come back."

"Let me see," Betty said, pushing Cecile out of the way. Betty stood on her toes and looked in as Cecile sat on the stairs and began to cry. Betty stared at the untouched apartment for a while and then joined Cecile on the steps. She also cried and they held each other for a long time.

"I'm afraid Mama and Papa are gone, Betty" Cecile said trying to hold back her grief. "They didn't come back from where the Germans took them. Neither did Marguerite or Grandmother and Grandfather. "

"What happened to them?" Betty asked.

"I think the Nazis killed them." There was a long, silent pause.

"I miss Mama and Papa."

"I miss them too, Betty."

"We'll never see them again."

"No, we won't. They probably went to heaven and helped us get away."

"I won't forget them, ever."

"No, Betty. No matter how wonderful the people are that we meet, we'll only have one Mama and Papa," Cecile said, both to Betty and to herself.

Again, they sat in silence for a long time, each in her own

thoughts.

"I think we should go now Betty."

"Alright. But I want to look in again," she got up and looked into the apartment.

After Betty walked away, Cecile looked in for the last time. "Good-bye for always Mama. Good-bye for always Papa. I love you. I will always look after Betty and I will always be your Shepali." She turned and walked quickly down the steps and into the street where the director was waiting for them.

She knew right away what they found. In fact, she knew before they got there. But the girls had to be given the opportunity to feel the terrible reality for themselves. She had been through this other times with some of the other children. It was a moment she hated, but one she knew had to take place.

"There was no one home, was there?" she asked tenderly.

"No. We could see in and nobody ever came back," Cecile said.

"I was afraid of that," the director said.

"Did they get killed?" Betty wanted to know.

"No one knows for sure. But I'm afraid there's a very good chance they did."

Betty took a deep breath and tears streamed down in the exhale. Cecile just stood in front of her house in silence.

"I think we should go home now," the director said quietly. The girls got into the car, their eyes glued to the window of their apartment as it sped away. They kept looking until the director turned the corner.

It took many days for Cecile to get over seeing the apartment she grew up in. It seemed every time she closed her eyes, a wonderful scene of her parents and sisters laughing and hugging would come to mind. However, each time it was quickly replaced by the cold, frightening vision seen from the outside of the door.

She was very confused about her feelings of seeing the apartment. Everything was there. The apartment was complete, with one exception, there were no people. Still a young girl, Cecile longed more than anything, for the warmth and safety she felt with her Papa, Mama and sisters. But while the look into the apartment gave her some of that recollection, it also served to rip those memories from her. For three years she held out hope that her family would be reunited. It was, after all, at least possible, that her parents could have gotten out and returned to Paris. But the undisturbed apartment was like the closing of a hard steel door on the memories and hope she held so closely to her heart.

When Cecile and Betty were to leave the orphanage for America, the other children made them a party. They were given a present of a book of pictures of the months they had spent together. It was a beautiful gift and represented a happy time for Betty and Cecile.

The girls went by train to LeHavre where they joined 70 other orphans on a ship called the Athos 2. They were led aboard the ship and placed in a lower section without staterooms. They slept in hammocks in an open area during their 15 day voyage to New York and their new home. After an uneasy beginning, filled with fear and loneliness, they made friends with the other children. They played on the ship, often running wildly about. They shared their stories of tragedy, escape and triumph. Mostly though, Cecile and Betty wondered what their new life was going to be like.

As the Athos 2 steamed closer to New York Harbor, the girls ran on deck. In the distance, New York City rose from the sea.

"We're in America, Betty. We're in America."

Cecile couldn't help but be impressed by the world emerging in the distance. The new world, which always represented freedom to all who longed for that privilege, was looming.

Betty understood less about freedom, but knew all about excitement. She peppered her sister with an endless array of questions.

"What's that Cecile?"

"That's the Statue of Liberty. The land of the free and the home of the brave." She had read all about it. "That's where Katz lives and Max and the Doctor and us." What a wonderful feeling Cecile had. She was in America. She stared out at the New York skyline and closed her eyes for a moment. She grabbed her little bag and held it tight. She thought of Memere and Pepere, and Father Louis. She thought of their train ride to Normandy and the invasion that saved them. She thought of the farmer and his wife and the sad German soldier who came to the house. She thought of running through the fields and of the poor dog. But when all those thoughts were gone, she came to Mama and Papa and Marguerite. Mama was right, Cecile thought. She was always there to help them. She was always there to guide them through any danger. She would be with them as long as Cecile and Betty were alive. "Thank you Mama. Thank you Papa. Thank you Marguerite. I will never forget you."

She took hold of Betty's hand as the ship slowly steamed towards their new beginning. The lump in her throat wouldn't go away and the chill in the air only heightened her sense of anticipation. After all she had been through, Cecile was looking forward to being a little girl again.

EPILOGUE

Herz and Marguerite Widerman died in the Auschwitz concentration camp. The Nazis transported the Jews from the Velodrome D'hiver to a holding detention center at Drancy, where they were loaded onto trains for the trip to the death camp.

Laja Widerman was nursed back to health and taken to Auschwitz where she was also killed.

Henri and cousin Robert died in Auschwitz.

Cecile and Betty's grandparents and their aunt's family were taken away the night the girls left with Memere and died in Auschwitz.

Three of the children in Memere's care found their parents after the war.

One of the children, Jacquot, Cecile and Betty's first cousin, came to live with Memere in Normandy. He lives in Paris with his wife. Cecile and Jacquot are in touch and saw each other a short time ago.

One of the others, Sami, emigrated to Israel, where he died in the Israeli army before his 20th birthday.

The other two remained with Memere and Pepere. Eventually, they all moved into a very poor neighborhood back in Paris. The Boisgointiers were given 1700 francs after the war from O.S.E. for their role in keeping the chil-

dren alive. The money went very fast and they never were able to move from an apartment in a Parisian slum.

Cecile Widerman Kaufer went back to Normandy to visit Memere in 1963. Memere was very old and very ill by then. When Cecile arrived Memere told her she had been waiting for years for her to return. She told Cecile how proud she was of her and how much she loved her. As sick as she was, she told Cecile she had prayed that she could stay alive until Cecile returned.

She died two weeks after Cecile's visit. Pepere and Rene' stopped answering Cecile's correspondence and their whereabouts are unknown.

Aunt Helene is still alive and lives in Paris.

Betty Widerman Carp is married, has two children, and lives in Houston.

Cecile Widerman Kaufer lives in Rockland County, New York. Now divorced, she lives close to her four children and nine grandchildren. Each day she kisses the pictures of her Mama, her Papa and her Sister hanging in her living room.

*T*his book is
dedicated to the children
of the Holocaust and the
brave heroes, simple,
ordinary people,
who risked everything to
help save their lives.
It is also dedicated to the
survivors of the period,
who have struggled to find
ways to live productive
lives after the tragedy
of Nazism.
Most of all, this book
is dedicated to the six
million victims—
fathers, mothers, grandfathers,
grandmothers, brothers,
sisters, aunts, uncles, cousins
and friends who will live on,
cherished forever
in our memories.